The Queen B

The struggle is real.
So is the comeback.

*an anthology of stories written by inspirational women on
their struggles, their comebacks & their commitment
to putting themselves first*

Arranged By

GINA CLAPPROOD

GINA CLAPPROOD

DEDICATION

This book is dedicated to all of the beautiful souls that shared a piece of themselves for this anthology.

The support I have received from my first two books has been humbling. The new connections I've made and the feedback that came as a result of them has been such an unexpected gift.

I had no intention to take on a third book, but divine intervention had other plans - which I will save for you to read about in my chapter.

Many of the contributors to 'The Queen B' shared their connection to my books and how much they could also relate. As they shared their truths with me, I knew I was on to something bigger than myself, and I was not alone in living my own truth.

It is amazing to me that most of these women, when approached to contribute to this book, didn't feel that they had a story to share, or a story that was even worth sharing. As you read each chapter, you will too realize that not only do they have inspiring stories we can relate to, but that you too, are not alone and you never know who you could inspire.

We all have struggles. We all have times in our lives where we feel we just want to give in and give up. The stories shared throughout these pages have one commonality—think of yourself, don't settle and don't you dare give up. Regroup, and refocus on YOU and your authenticity. You will have struggles. And you will persevere with a comeback. Think of that comeback and let it motivate the hell out of you!

I cannot thank these 30 women enough for sharing their inspiring stories. I will be forever be grateful to you all.

Thank you. xo

Table of Contents

The Queen B Contributors:

1 GINA CLAPPROOD | THE STRUGGLE + THE COMEBACK

"Life is not about the amount of days you live, but the amount of life in your days" – MAP

"How do you do it all? You are so inspiring. I could never do everything you do, Gina, without going completely out of my mind. How do you find the time?!"

Right. These are the words I often hear. Believe me, I get it. I understand I may seem like an overachiever to many, but I can assure you, I am not. Although I am a Virgo and we are known for getting shit done, I swear I don't set out to have a million things going on at once. I just try to compartmentalize and keep myself busy—to preserve my own sanity. As you may know by now, I wrote two books in 2018 and didn't tell a single soul until the first was approved to be published. I had always said I wanted to write a book before I turned thirty. Well, thirty came and went and I found myself having just turned forty, with the same, if not more, amount of stress than the previous ten years.

I wrote the books not for the purpose of crossing off my bucket list, but because I needed an outlet. I needed a voice because I was constantly listening to everyone else's. I found myself repeatedly advising my clients to put themselves first in relationships, go after what they wanted at work, color their hair purple if it was going to make them feel like the beauty, they were…and to just be happy. I felt like such a hypocrite because I was so stressed out and doing nothing to take care of myself.

For the last eight years my family had struggled mostly in silence. Only close family and friends were aware of the hell that was going on inside the walls of our home. We had an unwanted visitor that took up residence unexpectedly - we called him 'Shithead'.

'Shithead' is what we so appropriately named my son's OCD. *(*I refer to the OCD as Shithead instead of naming my son here because I don't want my feelings towards his OCD, to in any way be misconstrued for my feelings towards my son. I have to view the two as separate entities -and compartmentalize Shithead as best I can. I struggled with whether or not to write about this part* *of my life for a while out of fear of disapproval of any kind. I finally decided to write about this because it is my truth...and has spanned over such a long period of time in our lives. If I didn't write about this part of my life, I would not feel as though I was being true to myself and the journey that has gotten me to where I am today. Rest assured that this story is being written with my son's full permission. His hope is that it will help someone else suffering with OCD know to not give up on overcoming it. I hope that if you are dealing with your own 'Shithead', especially with someone in your own home, that you know you are not alone and there is a light at the end of what seems like a very long and dark tunnel.)*

Back to 'Shithead', my poor son was diagnosed with OCD in the 4th grade, but Shithead reared his ugly head a couple years prior, he was just a bit more subtle in the very beginning before making his grand entrance.

Shithead wasn't your typical type of OCD centered around cleanliness or counting. No, this Shithead was focused on just our house and the fact that it was always "a mess". My house was never a "mess" but to Shithead, if we had mail on the countertops, a glass on the table, our shoes off and placed near a door, etc. -it was a "mess" and had to be cleaned. So, Shithead would take control and shove the mail wherever he could find a space, whether logical or not, a closet, drawer, etc. Shithead would move the glasses we were drinking out of, that still had our drink in them, into the sink. Our shoes were thrown down the basement stairs. Shithead would approve of nothing being out in plain sight. Our house had to look pristine in his eyes—nothing could be in view that made it look 'messy'.

Apparently, there were birthday parties we were invited to that we missed and never even knew about because the invitation got shoved away somewhere. Bills came that we didn't know about, that was hard one to explain. Closets and drawers were constantly jam packed with all sorts of stuff that Shithead didn't feel like seeing. It didn't matter how messy the areas were that he couldn't see—closets, the basement, drawers, under the cabinets, etc.— those were left for me to deal with cleaning out and recleaning, weekly. We were prisoners in our own home and at the mercy of this unwanted guest.

I became more sensitive when someone around me would happen to make a comment that they were "a little OCD" or that they would love to have someone with OCD clean their house for them. It was all I had to bite my tongue. But I get it, there is a part of me that gets the humor and would never jump down someone's throat about such comments, but let me make it clear -I can assure you, if you were in my shoes, you would pray to be able to clean your own house and wouldn't wish OCD upon your worst enemy.

We tried everything over the years to abolish Shithead. I was against medication in the beginning and was convinced to try a natural supplement that was sure to work based on results with others. It worked so well that within days of taking it, there was no sign of Shithead. We were thrilled to have a semblance of normalcy back. We were even more thrilled that my son was able to get his life back. This lasted about over a year. Out of nowhere though, Shithead started visiting us again. To my dismay, I learned that the formulation of the supplement was changed and apparently was no longer effective in keeping Shithead away.

As a result, Shithead came back with a vengeance. I put aside my feelings about medicating my son and saw a therapist who recommended a psychiatrist for medication options. This doctor prescribed a medication and overnight, Shithead had left the building. OVERNIGHT. It was amazing. It was also too good to be true as my son's fifth grade teacher called me one day a month later and said that my son didn't seem like himself. He was disruptive in class—which was the polar opposite of his normal reserved behavior. He seemed to have no filter all of a sudden as well. The doctor took him immediately off this medication and every medication trial after that was unsuccessful.

As a mom, you would do anything for your child. No matter what. I couldn't bear to watch my son trapped by these obsessions and compulsions and I refused to accept this as his life. I spent countless hours researching possible treatment options, joined groups for OCD on social media, etc., I even had his name on a wait list for a well-known intensive treatment program as a last resort.

I would work all day and dreaded coming home because as soon as

I entered the house, I would see my husband's frustrated face, watching Shithead cautiously moving around our kitchen table and straightening it over, and over, and over, and over again. Shithead would yell at us when we went to sit at that same table for dinner because he had just gotten it into the 'perfect position'. And by "yell" I mean a meltdown of epic proportions that would last for hours. The stress was unbearable.

Summers were so much worse because the routine of school and being out of the house wasn't happening. Instead, Shithead was in the house all day and had a vice grip hold on my son. He would have to make sure things were perfect inside the house before even stepping foot outside to play with his friends. It was heart wrenching. Vacations and any little getaways we had to try to relax, were overshadowed by Shithead accompanying us, pictures from our vacation would show us as one happy family, when behind the scenes we were stressed out of our minds.

My husband and I have been together since high school, we have always been able to keep things light and try to laugh even in the most stressful of times. We did our best to remain true to this, but we were experiencing A LIVING HELL and we were stressed, exhausted and losing that lightheartedness.

One day, Shithead became verbally abusive towards me. He was frustrated that I kept taking him to doctor's appointments and therapy. He felt he needed to be discharged from those visits because according to him, he was fine, and his behavior was perfectly rationalized. As months went on, I learned to not react as much as possible to the verbal attacks and let me tell you, they were like a knife that went right to the heart—but that only lasts so long before you go inward. There were countless nights I would cry myself to sleep or have a good cleansing cry in the shower to kick off my day because I didn't know what else to do and didn't want anyone to see me crumble, because I had it all together right?! I was afraid to show that I was losing it out of fear that of what may happen if I gave into the stress.

In 2014 life threw us the best curveball. To my surprise, I learned I was pregnant with my 3rd son. The age gap would be between my oldest son of 10 years, and my now middle son of 8 years. I was excited and stressed because I worried about the environment this baby would be born into. I prayed that a new baby would be the distraction we needed and that our house would be way too crowded for Shithead to want to stay. I was wrong. DEAD WRONG. Shithead staked his claim even firmer once the baby arrived and was so not happy about the baby gear and toys everywhere. Life got more and more stressful and we did all we could to maintain some sort of normalcy for the sake of the baby. My middle son had now also started to withdraw to his room more and more to avoid the chaos.

At this time, we were referred to a new therapist. The therapy didn't help because Shithead was so manipulative, he would tell the therapist what he wanted to hear and then go back home and continue about his normal obsessive routine. We also continued to try medications-this time with a new doctor, because the previous doctor pretty much decided that the OCD must be caused by US since it only occurred when we were alone with him at home, or when Shithead was out alone with us, and nothing else was working. There was a lot of trial and error, but nothing seemed to really work. This was now our new normal, but I refused to throw in the towel and give up on my son - or my sanity.

■■

They say there are moments in your life that define you. Change you. Leave you by the wayside and never come back to get you.

The moments that leave you changed. FOREVER.

My son had a special bond with my stepfather, Michael. Michael didn't have a good (or any) relationship with his own sons so when my first son was born, he was the first grandchild, and I feel in many ways, he saw my son as his 'comeback'. Michael knew of our struggles, he had struggles of his own and would often spend time with my son and try to get him to open up and understand that he wasn't alone in this.

On Christmas Day 2014, Michael told me he was going to take my son for a walk and let him know that he was always there for him to talk to. This was after Shithead had barricaded himself in the closet because he couldn't handle that Christmas dinner was at our house and everything was out of its place for the holiday festivities.

My son seemed calmer when he got back from their walk, and Michael let me know that he told my son that he would be there for him, pick him up and take him out whenever he needed and was only a phone call away.

A month later, the exact moment that I can reference as my defining moment, I received a call from my mom that Michael had collapsed while walking from their backyard to the front of the house after a snowstorm and was being rushed to the hospital unresponsive.

In that moment, I aged lifetimes.

I am the oldest daughter, and my sister had just had my niece a few weeks prior, so I naturally went into some kind of 'let me handle everything mode'. I refused to leave my mother's side as we pleaded with the team of doctors for any sign of hope, for what seemed like an eternity, had been only a week. I had never experienced the passing of someone in that state, never mind someone you had always known as the person that could walk into a room, light it up with his vibrance and make you feel instantly at ease. To watch this person in such a lifeless pathetic state was the most heart wrenching tragedy I had ever witnessed, coupled with the fact that my mother-whom he adored and still called his "Bride", was now preparing for the worst.

The worst would solidify on the date of February 4, 2015.

It was during this time that something 'snapped' in me. It's hard to explain exactly, but the way I thought about everything changed drastically. I quickly changed into a woman that no longer worried what people thought, what they would think, etc. Life has a way of putting things in perspective very quickly and changing your priorities entirely.

Michael would always say to me- "it's not about the amount of days in your life, it's about the amount of life in your days". I can say with absolute certainty that he strived to live his life to the fullest. My mom was so happy and in love with him and while I still cry like a baby as I sit here and type this story, I am so happy to know that my mom was blessed with the years she did have with Michael, because I know so many of us never find that kind of love or adoration, or have the opportunity to travel together as they did and truly enjoy life as it should be enjoyed.

Some people believe in divine intervention, some don't. I am a BELIEVER. When I had some time alone with Michael in his final days, I would like to believe that in some way he heard me ask him, plead with him, to please continue to help me with my son. I was so worried about my son going on a downward spiral after such a big part of his support system, as promised, was being ripped away from him.

My son's OCD reached its worst peak after Michael's passing and I remember pulling into the parking lot at work months later one summer morning, on the verge of tears and just thinking to myself, "Please, if there is anything, ANYTHING, I am missing, please give me a sign to help him". It was then that the thought of calling my Chiropractor's office literally popped into my head.

I composed myself and called right then from the car. I spoke with them about what I was struggling with with my son. Dr. Ed probably heard the desperation in my voice and told me that they could fit my son in for an appointment that afternoon. When I arrived, my son was to see Dr. Judy, who I swear, took the time to figure out what the core of the issue was. For instance, was something causing Shithead that we didn't realize-such as diet, allergies, EMF, poor gut health, etc.? She did this detox foot bath on him, and overnight Shithead was gone. GONE.

The crazy divine intervention that happened here? Michael was a chiropractor.

He was loved by his patients and he too believed in treating the whole person holistically as well as through traditional medicine. I couldn't believe that in all my hours of research, and my own personal success with chiropractic care, that I never once even thought of chiropractic care as a possible option in treating my son! I was also completely unaware of the various types of treatments this office offered, that were outside of what is typically known as chiropractic care.

At one point I didn't care if she was doing voo-doo, if it was working, I was all for it! She was somehow holistically figuring it out and my son was vastly improving. I will always believe the thought that popped into my head that morning to call their office was Michael's divine intervention.

My son made a huge change in about six months under their care and Shithead wasn't around as intensely. Life was bearable again. As my son got a little older and what I believe was due to hormonal changes at thirteen, Shithead started to come around a bit more. And more. Before it was to get any more intense, I decided to take him back to his doctor and advocated for him to go back on the very first medication, the one that was too strong for him back in the fifth grade that gave him the side effect of being 'too social' and having no filter. At this point I would rather have that, than the alternative. I felt that if it were too strong for him years ago, perhaps with his growth spurt and any hormonal changes, it should be worth another shot, because it had been the one and ONLY medication that worked for him at all.

The doctor could tell that I was at my breaking point and I was not going to budge. I kept having this inkling that holistic therapy coupled with this med would be a solution. She honored my desperation and 'mother's intuition' and I am happy to say that the lowest dose of this medication worked and has been 100% effective since. Shithead is no longer having a foot hold on my son or my family.

I wrote my first book during this time as an outlet because I knew I needed something to focus on in order to keep my sanity because my whiskey old fashioneds could only help so much. Soon after publishing my first, I wrote my second book. Right before the release of this book, I went to see a medium. When I sat down with her, she immediately told me that Michael was there in the room and that "he is so proud that you are an author. He said you are not done though, there is another book coming, that others are going to relate to. It is going to inspire so many others. Watch for the signs." He also told her that he "heard what I said to him in the hospital and promised he was always by my son's side". I was floored. I told the medium my second book was releasing soon, and she told me that Michael was referring to a third book while communicating with her.

A few nights after my session with this medium, I had a dream. It was SO VIVID. It was the first time I had dreamt of Michael in so long and he was showing me my next book. He was turning the pages and at the end of each page I was shown, I saw: "I am a Boss", "I am a Bitch", "I am a Selfish B", "I am a Believer". This book seemed to be a collection of stories written by women who identified with putting themselves first.

A few nights later, I had a second dream, I was standing on a platform or stage, a lit screen of some kind behind me, and I said to an audience, "The struggle is real, so is the comeback", and this jolt went through me and I felt it with every fiber of my being. I get chills and tears every time I think back to it as it was that strong. I looked out into the audience and in the front row were my grandmothers (the inspiration for my second book), applauding and smiling, and right next to them, was Michael, standing, smiling and cheering me on.

So, as I alluded to in my 'Dedication' above, I had no plans to write this book. This book is a result of my dreams. It is a result of the fact that I was told by Michael through divine intervention that I wasn't done writing. It is a result the inspiration I felt from the beautiful souls who shared their stories with me. It is a result of not only my struggle with my son, my son's struggles with OCD, my mom's struggles with becoming a widower for a second time, but it is a result of the comeback. The determination to keep at it despite the struggle and know that there is hope and healing ahead for all of us.

I was compelled to release this book on the same date of Michael's passing to honor him, celebrate his life and all the struggles up through this point. I wanted to somehow show him that I received his messages loud and clear. I am motivated to make one hell of a comeback, for my son, my family, friends, for his memory, and for myself.

I am finally in a place where life has calmed down a bit, not entirely, but isn't that what life is? Beautiful chaos. Ugly challenges. Struggles to tackle, and comebacks to inspire. Shithead is gone, my son is doing great, he is on the honor roll and ironically participating in a work readiness program through his high school where he works at the Chiropractic Office with Dr. Judy a couple days a week! If Shithead ever decides to pay us another visit, I know that I am in good hands when it comes to sending him packing.

I am finally at a point in my life where I feel that I have earned the right to put myself first without apology. I purposely take time to myself to decompress and refresh. I used to be more high strung, now I am much more relaxed and don't assume things based on my own perspective—I have learned to keep things real and talk things through versus the opposite. I don't overreact and I don't let things bother me because in the grand scheme of things, I have witnessed how life can change in an instant and is truly fragile. Now when I come home from work to a gloriously 'messy' house and can sit at the kitchen table without consequence, I don't take that for granted. I have learned how stressful life can be, but also how amazing it can be as well. I have learned how to navigate through struggles without giving up on the end goal or losing my complete self. I have earned my rightful place as one of these amazing Queen B's.

I am a Believer.

2 KATE D. | ALLOW ME TO REINTRODUCE MYSELF

"Hi, I'm Kate - I gained 100 lbs. in just over a year, had a mental breakdown, have severe depression, severe anxiety and suffer from agoraphobia. Nice to meet you."

This has been my introduction when meeting people for the past five years of my life. I didn't have an identity; my circumstances were what described me, and I made sure to let others know. Why? Because if they found out some other way, or if I was a little off, they knew why. This would DEFINITELY make you want to be my friend, right?!

Five years ago, I would say I was living the life. I had just moved back from NYC (loved it, but financially...not so much), and landed a great job that I truly loved. When you have a job, you LOVE waking up for every day, it's a game changer. Fast forward a few months into my job and I found myself in a horrible situation. I was having an affair with my CEO. Granted, he said he was splitting up with his wife and even got his own apartment, but it's something I never ever should have gotten involved in. This went on for a while, until he told me he was going home. Wait...what? I was 11 years younger than him and his assistant...the situation was already horrible. After he ended up moving home, things just escalated. I was forced to see him every day, knowing things were done and I was supposed to put on a happy face. From my side, it was impossible. The worst was when his wife would come into the office, and he saw nothing wrong with that (yes, I know they're married, but I was led to believe a different story only to see none of it was true).

Now here's where things get really messed up. He went home, I get heartbroken, but he still wants to keep a sexual relationship. Me being the young naive girl I am, was excited about this, but not the cheating aspect. I was still so hurt that I wasn't good enough and he made sure I knew it. Constantly telling me about his home life, things they do together, etc. It was brutal. However, there was a time where I was forced to do the sexual things...or I'd lose my job. A job I built a life around and would lose an awful lot financially without, and I wouldn't find something else with that salary in a long time, if at all. He had officially put his power over me and knew I was in a corner and couldn't get out.

I spent every single day crying. Crying over the fact that I'm not good enough, that I'm being forced to do things I don't want to do so I can maintain the life I have, forced to put on a smile so no one knows what's going on and he doesn't lose his company. Crying because WTF am I doing and how did I get here?!

I finally broke and had a mental breakdown. I couldn't handle the stress I was under and just wanted everything to go away, including my life. I took the necessary steps to check myself into a rehab center to get some mental help, so I could get back on my feet again and not suffer the way I had been. There's such a stigma around mental health issues and being institutionalized, and taking medication, etc., but let me tell you, my inpatient experience was one of the best experiences of my life. It humbled me and the workers made me realize it's NOT me, it's a chemical thing, it's circumstances, it's so many other factors but me, myself...I'm ok, I just couldn't see it.

After leaving there I went back to work thinking everything was fine, although everyone was telling me to look for another job. I told just about every single person to F off, I can handle it. I couldn't afford to get another job, so I had to suck it up. Worst. Decision. Ever.

Over the next few months I lost myself. I became this incredibly angry person that was happy being mad. I wanted to make others feel like I did as well, and I made sure I did just that. I did this in the workplace because even still, he had sexual control over me. I was mad I was right back where I was a few months prior, I was still in the stupid situation I got myself into, and I couldn't get ahold of myself. Things came to a head when he came to my house one day and brought someone I worked with, who I was very good friends with, to talk about things going on with me. I didn't want to lose my cool on them so I popped some Klonopin that I was prescribed so I could instantly calm down and deal with it. The minute they got there, she came in and physically jumped on me and straddled me on the couch, hitting me. All I could think is "HOLY SHIT WHAT IS GOING ON?!" By this point I was too relaxed to try and defend myself, and just couldn't do it. I had asked them to leave numerous times only to be told no. I then said I was going to call the police and got a response of "what good is that going to do for you?". I was enraged, and my head was SPINNING. I was trapped in my own home.

I got up, barefoot, and walked out my front door and started walking down the street trying to get my head together and figure out what in the hell was happening. I then said to myself, "why am I leaving MY house?" ...so, I went back to the house, went into the kitchen and got a butter knife. I stood in the doorway across the room from them, nowhere close to anyone with ZERO intention of hurting anyone, and said "seriously, LEAVE". The girl flipped out, went outside, and called the police on me. Soon after, the police showed up, then a fire rescue, and I was sent to be institutionalized...again. This time, it wasn't my choice. This started my severe downward spiral because from that inpatient stay onward, I lost my job and she got to keep hers, and I was left to feel like a complete piece of shit. He sat there and watched her attack me and did NOTHING to help. I could see him out of the corner of my eye just sitting there watching. Do you know how that feels? Someone you thought was on your side for everything, watching you be hit by someone who then has you sent away to a mental hospital? From that point on, I just gave up on myself in every sense of the word.

I was given a one-year severance because honestly, I could have taken his whole company down. I spent that year trying to get myself better and thinking that I was. I was trying to convince myself that I was doing so much better, things didn't bother me anymore, I'm better than that, etc. but I still wasn't ok. I was crying all the time, my head would replay that incident over and over again, every siren I heard I was convinced they were coming for me...I was living in my own personal hell. I ended up getting treated for depression, anxiety and PTSD because this was officially consuming my life. I've always struggled with being in a public setting because I don't like people looking at me and judging me (I don't think I'm attractive, and I hate that people have to see me...even to this day), but since that incident I became AFRAID of leaving the house.

What was I scared of? Getting sent to a hospital against my will, running into anyone from my previous job because I knew they had all been told what happened (she went back and quickly told everyone - how great), being judged and feeling like a psycho...when I know I'm not. Everyone had this image of me that was painted for them by other people that just wasn't who I was and there was no convincing otherwise. So, I stayed in my house and didn't leave. It started slow at first - going out to a friend's house a few times a week, staying in the rest. Going to the store twice a week - staying home the rest. This went on for at least 10 months.

At one point, I was at a friend's house and met her and her husband's roommate and we clicked. He expressed interest and I was SO. FRIGGEN. HAPPY. Someone who liked me after all the mental anguish I went through? This is impossible, or so I thought. We hit it off, ended up dating, and it was great. I should say, "great".

I'll never regret dating him, and we did for 2.5 years, but there's so much I wish was different on both of our parts...but mainly me. Having him around allowed me to give up 100% and let him do everything. I then became so agoraphobic that I did not leave the house AT ALL for well over a year, I wasn't taking care of myself or my environment, I just didn't care. I ended up gaining 100 lbs. in just over a year because of how much I gave up and was homebound. That's RIDICULOUSLY hard to deal with, especially when you're already going through tough situations mentally. But he loved me, I just stopped knowing how to love at all.

I'll always appreciate everything he did for me, but we had our issues for sure. About a year after dating, we bought a house together and I got a job. These were HUGE steps for me and I was so damn proud of myself. This job though, was $20,000 less than my other job. I thought I could make it work especially with him helping out - until he didn't help out. I ended up being the sole provider for us, while he would say "I paid for dinner last night!", "I always buy the dog food! Don't say I don't do shit!", etc. I never knew how to respond and felt like I was wrong all the time, so I always thought he was right, and I shouldn't be questioning him. When we split up, I found myself in $85,000 worth of debt and no idea how I was going to repay it.

No one understand stress until they literally can't afford to put gas in their car or put food in their fridge. The level of stress I've experienced having no money is like none I've ever experienced before. I was making gooood money before and never had to worry about a price tag, so going from that to nothing is HARD. When you're used to living one way, coming down from it isn't easy, especially when you still have the bills following you from that income. After our breakup, I decided enough is enough - something needs to change because nothing is changing. I was so upset about our breakup that I couldn't see straight, but after two weeks I calmed down. The storm settled. That's when I came to and said, "let's get this ball rolling". I don't know what happened, but damn am I happy it did.

I decided to reach out to friends I hadn't spoken to in years because he and I isolated ourselves. Granted, some still don't want much to do with me, but I apologized and said what I had to say because I was wrong. When I'm wrong, I'll admit it, and I felt like it was time to do that. From there, I decided to get a life coach to work through all of these areas of my life that were in shambles. I needed help organizing everything and putting the pieces back together so I could live like a more normal, functioning, human-being. I stumbled upon the BEST person for me, and I will always, 1000%, be grateful for her. I started seeing her in April, one month after my breakup, and I don't know what happened, but I had a complete mental shift. One day I woke up, and things were going to be okay! I decided I wasn't going to live the life I had been, and I'm going to put my fears aside and start living. She made me realize things I didn't realize about myself, and boy did that put things into perspective for me.

I started going out by myself, even if just to the store, which I hadn't done in at least 3 years. I had a feeling of determination to get things done and get my life back on track, I started to feel better about myself, and most of all, I started to learn that I can love myself and that's okay to do. Once these things started to happen for me, I noticed people were gravitating back to me like they used to years before, I noticed I was able to at least text more people and had a feeling of being wanted again. I felt like a nobody and unwanted for so long that I forgot what it felt like, and damn did it feel good.

Most of all, she pushed me to start chasing what I want in life. I'm not very happy in my current job and don't feel valued or competent. I don't dislike it, but I know I can find better, and I think I can find better for more money (you know, so I can live?). Looking for a new job has not been on my radar in at least 5 years. There's no way! How could I, miss agoraphobic that couldn't leave the house and lost her social skills, interview for a new job? Interviewing is about selling yourself, and I had nothing to sell. We spent time going through my resume and comparing the work experience I had to what people were looking for...and I was eligible for a lot more than I thought I was. I couldn't see just how good I am, but she made sure I did. The more we talked about it, the more intrigued I became. Could I get a new job? Could I make more money? Could I afford my bills, gas and food again?

GINA CLAPPROOD

Bankruptcy was knocking at my door, so I decided why the hell not try. I put my resume up on the job search sites hoping someone would reach out to me and within a few days I got a call from a recruiter. I ended up going on three rounds of interviews with a company that would have helped me so much financially, but the position went to another candidate, unfortunately. However, this made me realize that I've got it! I CAN do this. I went through three rounds of interviews and it was between me and one other person. Your girl sold herself...because she felt like she finally had something to sell. On to the next one!

I'm still out there looking, interviewing, and working with my life coach because I'm getting what I want dammit. I'm finally chasing what I want, and I'm not settling. I've spent too much time focusing on what others think of me, focusing on what's wrong with me, focusing on how I got in this terrible position, thinking about if I'll ever find anyone to love me again... it's all so tiring and I wore myself out. I'm beyond happy to say that I finally have my depression under control with the help of therapy and medication, my anxiety is MUCH less than it was with the help of therapy and medication, and I'm INCREDIBLY HAPPY to say that I'm able to leave my house on a daily basis, go to the store if needed, and break free from the shackles I put on myself. Even better? I've lost 83 lbs. over the past 9 months because this determination is back and I'm getting myself back. I'm finally ready to tackle this thing called life.

"Hi, I'm Kate - and I'm a **Boss Ass Bitch,** allow me to reintroduce myself."

3 JEN SENECAL | THE DREAM

When I was a little girl, I couldn't wait to be a grown-up. I wanted the American Dream: graduate college, land a killer job, find the man of my dreams, get married, have kids, live happily ever after in my white picket-fenced house with two dogs, 6 weeks of vacation time and a loaded 401K. And, God willingly, all before I turned 30.

Isn't that what we all wanted? The perfect blueprint. The prep plan that was embedded into our DNA from an early start. The life layout that would bring endless joy, happiness, and impeccably beveled crown molding (who knew there were so many?). Somehow, we even managed to tie our self-worth and placement in the world to how quickly and efficiently we mastered this. If you landed the Dream, you made it.

I did find the Dream. I graduated from Providence College with a degree in Biology and secured a decent job shortly after. I found the man of my dreams, who also gave me a lucrative business together, three beautiful daughters, a house, a home, stock options, vacations to Disney and a level of comfort that anyone would be crazy to ever give up. I had gone ahead and found myself a good life with the man I love, just like I always wanted. All before I was 30.

So, how did I end up divorced, completely lost and confused, and starting my entire life over a decade later?

I've asked myself this question no less than 42,000 times. While the answer is a book in itself, I've realized that, in its most simplified form, somewhere along the way I forgot who I was. I became a victim to my own American Dream, and not because the Dream did anything wrong to me, but because I victimized myself within it. I took the Dream that was granted to me and I made it the enemy. I thought that since I was giving myself over to the Dream, doing everything it wanted me to, sacrificing (self-diagnosed) day after day, that I should be happy. And when something was wrong with my happiness, I blamed the Dream. But what really happened is that I forgot. I forgot that the Dream doesn't work unless you stay true to who are the entire time, and not just play a role of who you think you're supposed to be. The Dream doesn't work when you stop being honest. Or when you start blaming it for your shortcomings. Or when you think you're the only one participating in it (even though you're not). Or even when you have a whole bunch of babies in a short amount of time and realize that motherhood is one of the most (if not THE most) wonderful things in the Dream but can also cripple you if you use it as a crutch to forgetting who you are, too.

Nope, it wasn't the Dream I was unhappy with. I was unhappy with myself.

My story isn't uncommon. There are thousands of women who could give you the same play-by-play. But we all have to ask ourselves collectively why it happens so often. How did we get here? What could we have done differently? And, most importantly, what is our Dream actually supposed to look like and how are we supposed to handle it? Because the one we all went to bed at night at age 12 dreaming about is breaking left and right.

After many sleepless nights of reflection, months of therapy, and endless sob-fests with friends and family, I am even more convinced that it's not the Dream. It's our reaction to it. It's the expectation we place upon it. And how we interact with our own self, as well as the other people sharing the Dream with us. If we do it right, the Dream will allow us to shine. If not, it can swallow us in a pit of contentment, except no one is content.

But who the hell knows how to do it the right way? There are no instruction booklets that come with the Dream. So, what happens is that all of us newbies go at it without our hands held, and, much like a child learning to walk, we fall. And we get hurt. And we even break. Not many people are comfortable with breaking, because the stigma of breaking is failure. And that's what I thought for a long time, when my husband and I broke. That we failed. How could two people who love one another, with three incredible children and a great life fail? It didn't seem possible. But, as they say, shit happens. No matter how hard we tried (and we tried hard), we broke.

The split from my husband was not an easy one. We were the best of friends for 16 years, building our lives and family together, traveling all over as a pair, always laughing with one another, and boasting at our ability to hold a conversation for hours without it stopping. On paper, we were perfect. And, while we will always hold love for each other and are great friends now, even if we are no longer husband and wife, the pain and anguish of our family rearranging its structure a year ago has been nothing short of an emotional rollercoaster. Not only has our life schedule taken a new form, but I have found myself being forced to stand on my own two feet and start over at 41, which, quite frankly, is no easy feat. I mean, who the hell am I now? What do I want to do with myself? How do I manage work and the kids and sports and school and making sure they still eat in between all this? Do I ask for help? But what if people think I'm a failure (again) if I need help? Will I ever shop at Whole Foods again? Who pays for the kids' college? Do I really need cable? How do I close a pool? Do I even like Benjamin Moore paint? Why am I always lying on the living floor in silence late at night, staring at nothing?

CAN SOMEONE DO OUR LAUNDRY?

I often think back to who I was before I was initiated into the Dream. I was the girl who COULD stand on her own two feet. The girl who worked her butt off since she was a child. The one who excelled in school, took the most ambitious courses in college, lived on her own, traveled, had big goals, and had a whole lotta fun doing it all. This is the person I was supposed to stay as, once I walked through those beautiful, tall and inviting gates (I think they were made out of marble) to the Dream. I was her for a while in there. But somewhere along the way, in between changing diapers and filling out endless school forms, I got too comfortable with excelling at one role, while slowly neglecting the rest.

I think that's what's supposed to happen in the Dream, though. You get assigned a very big role, like being a mother, and your job is to give every fiber of your being to that role. The love that permeates between you and your children's hearts is big and fierce enough that every single thing outside of it melts away. That's OK. That is how it should be. But, there's a tricky part. The tricky part is not getting stuck there. Everything should melt away for a short time, but then it should come back together again. It's this melting moment, where everything stays liquid, that I think a lot of people in the Dream just break.

Ask any married mother or woman you know why they aren't feeling fulfilled or entirely happy and you'll probably get the same answer (if they respond honestly). They got stuck. They melted. Like me, they gave everything they had to one piece of the Dream and then forgot about the rest. The problem with forgetting the rest is that it's then very easy to cast resentment and blame, and then you begin to live a life that doesn't align with who you truly are, and things fall apart.

While hindsight is 20/20, I wouldn't have changed my Dream for the world. But I would have most definitely navigated it differently. However, as a firm believer in things happening as they should, my divorce was a gigantic wake-up call and the biggest life lesson available to me. It forced me to find that girl I was before I let her melt and bring her back. It's launched a career for me that should have been done a long time ago. It's put a fire under my ass to do bigger and better with my dreams. It repaired my friendship with my husband. It improved my relationships with my family, friends and children, because I am no longer a shell of myself existing in the day-to-day. It taught my daughters that it's ok to struggle and fall, and then get back up. They have seen their mother laughing, loving hard, panicking even harder, hustling, and hiding near a tree in the backyard while cutting the lawn, sobbing her eyes out. They have seen their mother trying to put all the pieces back together again, and most of the time, half of those pieces are all over the place and THAT'S OK. Perhaps they've even learned how to go about their own Dream someday. Our children have bonded in the process, with each other and with each of us, and have also learned how to say things like, "I'm so proud of you," or "It's OK if it hurts right now because someday it won't," or even, "You're doing your best and that's all that matters." They've even learned how to apologize and forgive more than they've ever done before, and they wear their hearts on their sleeves for everyone to see. I know this is partly because their father and I continuously show love and friendship and allow them to see our struggles to an extent, but he and I wouldn't have gotten to this place had we not broken.

Divorce isn't the easy way out. Starting over, financially and independently, is incredibly challenging. Doing things on your own, without a companion, well, just kinda sucks sometimes. But, finding that person you once were—and even having some alone-time now to explore her—is exhilarating, exhausting, soul-filling, inspiring and, will, in the end, make you stronger.

If I could talk to the 25 years-old version of myself, the year my Dream was about to begin, (or any 25-year-old about to do the same), I would tell her to never get stuck. That she could have it all, if she stayed true to who she was and kept reaching big on her own. And to never get too comfortable with one role or rely on the Dream for her happiness.

I may cry more than I have in 41 years, but I smile just as much and I'm stronger now. I am the **Boss** of the new Dream ahead of me.

4 CAROLINE ZANI | I TOOK MY POWER BACK

"The wound is where the Light enters you." – Rumi

For me, life has been an interesting mix of pure love and sheer terror. I don't know how to explain it any other way, but it sure does make for interesting experiences. Born to hardworking parents, I was one of 4 children and loved nothing more than being lost in the shuffle. I'm Aquarius, quiet, left-handed, had "imaginary " friends, animal lover, empath and born during a Mercury retrograde. Ha! I was the perfect storm for what was to come.

Throughout school I daydreamed mostly and with a photographic memory, I never had to bring textbooks home or study. I was a solid B student because I put in no effort. I simply didn't see the point of school as it just cut into my horse time. The moment I got home from school, I went to the barn to clean, groom, ride and clean some more. I'd do anything to avoid being around too many people in a day. What I didn't realize then was that the energy I had to deal with from other people didn't resonate with my energy and they drained me. Horses gave me a different, ego-free energy. If you have a dog or cat, you know what I mean. They love openly no matter what - and expect nothing in return.

Becoming a mother at age 20, I took to the role immediately and enthusiastically. My, my how a child can change your life. Nothing was more important than my child who was, of course, absolutely perfect. I knew I was blessed from day one. I'm not saying it was easy raising her alone but if there was ever a child that made it easy, it was her. For the first 12 years anyway. Then she became the typical tween / teen and hated me, but she did it with passion and she did it consistently! What more could a parent want, right? She taught me so much about life and myself and for that I am so grateful.

The rape though...that was something I never expected. Probably like the sentence you just read - out of the blue and hard to place. It was a defining moment for me - one that splits time in two - the great before and after.

Like many women I was so stunned by the experience that I was just happy to survive it physically and I said nothing. Showering was all I wanted to do. Wash it away, make myself clean again, and once my skin was dry, I'd just carry on. And I did! I went to work the next day, even going to a meeting at the police department as part of a coalition that met there every month. Yes, I was fine, and I didn't need to deal with what had happened until of course I did.

So many lessons we must learn on our path. We don't always get to choose the way the lesson presents itself, but we get to choose how we confront or run from it. And quite honestly the running gets exhausting but, in my case, confronting just made the misery an endless riptide of injustice. And in the midst of pre-trial garbage (after two years of insanity in the "the system") I did the only thing I could - the only move that was in my power.

I called the DA's office and told them I was done. I needed to be done. They told me I was their only agreeable witness (the man who raped me had raped many women all over the country but the women, though they came forward, refused to make a formal statement). I was their ticket, I was the woman the DA's office had been waiting for. They informed me that I was now a hostile witness and would be forced to testify. I told them that they would be responsible for my death one way or another. I had felt my life was in danger since that fateful day of April 8th, 2010 and the thugs who were hired to follow me and take pictures of me everywhere, I went and approach my daughter on her college campus 60 miles away, call my mother and threaten to kill her daughter...they were allowed to continue. "The defense has a right to their own investigation by private investigators at their own expense." Interesting. So, either he would kill me, or I would have a heart attack. Either way, I told the DA, I'm done.

I TOOK MY POWER BACK.

Today, I am on the path I was probably always meant for. It took a life-altering moment (truly a moment) to change my life, my journey, the road I walk and the way I walk it *(*heels optional)*.

The book I wrote just prior to the rape became the salve I needed to heal. It "catapulted me to a different career and speaking work.

Women need the messages this book will have." These are the words Gina told me in a reading before I believed in readings.

Full circle and full disclosure, I am now a reader and have built quite a following out of it and my book was picked up by a publisher. I even have an agent. So, you see, everything does happen for a reason.

Surprises, miracles, God winks, serendipity, synchronicity. Call it what you will but just know that we all have these little bits of glitter sprinkled throughout the blueprint that is our life. Our story. Our song. Our dance. Our daydream.

Be grateful, be humble, be open, be forgiving, be loving, be persistent, be badass, be a B*tch.

Be.

Caroline E. Zani, M.Ed. | Author of **Piper, Once & Again**
www.carolinezani.com

5 MELISSA M. C. | TRUST 'THE VOICE'

"Believe in miracles, and you will find yours!"

I've learned that sometimes to get what you truly want, you need to let go of attachment to an idea. In my case it was finding "The One". The craziest and riskiest thing I ever did was walk away from a GOOD three-year relationship with a GOOD guy at the age of 29. It shocked everyone- It seemed to happen almost out of nowhere, at least to the outside world. But on the inside, I knew something was missing. It was kind of like have the winning lottery ticket, except it was off by one number. I tried to figure out what was missing, and oftentimes it was not even something I could put my finger on. I WISH I had a clear-cut answer as to why.

It all happened when I was on a Florida vacation with some great friends. I had time to clear my head and not think about anything. It is in those moments that all of the answers came. The message came loud and clear and strong, "It's time to leave him, Melissa". I couldn't justify doing it without a specific reason- something significant. It was, after all, a solid relationship. We didn't fight much, we looked like a good couple, we went out and had fun, we stayed in and I made dinners. We hosted parties, we even moved in together. As terrible as this sounds, though, I just feel like my soul needed more. He didn't light my soul on fire. Sure, I loved him. Sure, he was a terrific guy and most people would give anything to have a good guy like that. I'm not sure I was ever IN love, like the deep, soul explosion kind of way.

Sometimes I felt like we lived 2 separate lives- he traveled for work and was gone a lot. But the crazy thing is I liked that! It gave me time to do me- to go out swing and salsa dancing and do my yoga and see my friends. Whenever the future came up, he shied away. I felt like the lack of moving the relationship forward was missing, and if it was there it was almost like it was a chore. I didn't want to get engaged to someone because we had dated long enough to reach that milestone. I wanted to get engaged because this was my guy, the person the universe intended for me, and nothing would ever keep us apart.

I don't want to bore you with the all of the nitty gritty about why the relationship worked and why it didn't. What mattered is that out of nowhere I dropped a bomb on this guy. I mean, we were living together! I felt a tremendous amount of guilt from this. I wanted him to be ok. I wanted to take his pain away. Through the whole ordeal it was as if something was guiding me and leading me. Every time I wanted to be weak and get back together, it wouldn't let me. It was as if someone else was speaking through me, knowing just what to say to gracefully part our separate ways, in the most caring and delicate way.

If it wasn't for this thing, I would still be with him today most likely, and probably in an unhappy marriage. I needed this thing to push me to make this drastic change in my life. I was scared and empty and ashamed. Everyone thought I was insane to end this relationship. What I would say was the relationship was good, but it wasn't amazing, and I need AMAZING.

For two years I dated like you couldn't imagine. I had an excel spreadsheet and I tracked every guy I went on a date with – their name, how we met, what I liked and didn't like about them. You

wouldn't believe the number of guys on this spreadsheet! Let's

say I was very busy and dating for me was a serious part time job.

Some weeks I would have what I called "power weeks" and I

would line up three dates three nights in a row and at the end of the

week I would choose one to continue with, or none. I never dated

more than one at a time. If I saw someone a second time, I wasn't

lining up any other dates. Oftentimes I only went out with them

once. I was a serial dater and wasn't messing around. I was dating

to find my husband and the man who sets my soul on fire. I had

dated enough in my life to know what I wanted, and I knew quick,

probably within the first 5 minutes of the date. I was always polite

and had a good time on these dates, but often they would be on

what I called "the fade out plan"- they call me, I text back. They

text, I respond a day later, and then not again. I was a heartbreaker.

I got maybe two or three "stage three clingers" that had a terrible

time understanding that I didn't want to go on another

date (translation, I didn't want to marry them). It was nothing

personal guys, really. You are awesome, just not my guy.

I had a great time along the way and met some really stand up guys. I dated all kinds. I wouldn't say I had a type. I was more looking for a specific type of love or connection.

Someone who spoke my love language- words of affirmation and wanted to spend quality time with me and make me a true priority as I would do for them. I had all of the industries covered- finance, medical, pilot, docs, those in grad school, dance instructor, entrepreneurs. Some were extroverts, some were introverts, some were looking for serious relationships and others just wanted to have fun. Again, I was just looking for the right connection. Even my best friend suggested I give them a chance at another date before I banished them forever, but I needed to follow my gut.

Fast forward to the end of these two years, on my 31st birthday. I'm out to eat with my parents, brother and sister and law. We have a great dinner, and then I open up my birthday card from my parents. In it says, "We are so proud of how true you always are to yourself". Wow, this line really struck a chord with me. What happens next? I burst into tears. Like, sobbing, uncontrollable mess. All of a sudden in that moment, with my loved ones around me, I just felt the truth of my current situation. I didn't need to pretend life was amazing and serial dating was amazing. I let my guard down and the truth was I realized that although I would never have a hard time finding a date or a boyfriend, it was possible that I came into this world without signing up for a "One". Maybe I would never get married, never have children. In this moment I realized that. I knew I would never settle, and this was my reality. I could be alone.

By this point I was exhausted, giving pieces of myself to all of these men, all of these different personalities. Keeping everyone's story straight, who likes chocolate, who has the older sister, who I saw that movie with. At that moment, I realized I could be alone. I realized that was being true to myself, as the card reminded me. That night my brother and sister- in- law did what any good friends would do- they took me out and showed me a good time and let me know they were there for me. I felt something shift inside of me.

Something happened the next morning, I woke up and I had truly accepted my fate. Not pretending I was ok with it, not wanting to be ok with it, but truly found peace in the fact that I had a different story than the "average" person. I was meant to be single and would still rock this world. No marriage, no kiddos for me. I learned to love this story and I found a deep sense of strength in knowing that the only thing I needed in this world was me.

Fast forward to a week later. I went on a date with someone I started talking to online. Someone who reached out to me a day before my 31st birthday. His name was John and he guessed my Myers Briggs personality type from my profile! Anyone who knows me knows that I LOVE personality assessments and Myers Briggs is my favorite. He was speaking my language! I was excited to meet him but kept my expectations low. After all, odds are he is just another number on the spreadsheet. I met up with him after I taught a yoga class to martial artists. I showed up to the restaurant in my yoga getup, bouncing all around the seat. (I get a real surge of energy after teaching).

I can't believe how comfortable with him I was! His eyes put me right at ease and I wanted to open up. What stood out to me most is how PRESENT he was. He was really into everything I was saying. We just jived. He just took a licensing exam that very morning! Up until then he was studying a lot and didn't have enough time to devote to dating or a relationship- enough to satisfy this girl, whose love language is quality time.

So, the universe presented this man at the exact earliest time it would have worked. We made another date for 5 days later. We couldn't wait to see each other, we snuck in another date before then. We couldn't get enough of each other. Needless to say, I took myself off the market right after our first date. When my parents heard I went on a second date with John they said, "Oh my, he must be the one!" They were right.

A month later the same voice that told me to leave the last boyfriend also told me that John is the one. The rest is history, and we were engaged 10 months later on the very bench we shared our first kiss.

We now have 2 beautiful daughters, a cat, a home, and all the love in the world. If I never left Mr. Good, I would have never found Mr. Great! "Never settle" is my life motto. We all create our own life stories. I am so glad I took a detour when I was 29. I had no idea what the future held, but I was brave enough to take a gamble because I trusted "The voice".

May you always listen to your inner voice, and may you always know that you deserve not just good, but Great!

I am a Selfish B.

6 ELIZABETH DELAITSCH | NEW

PERSPECTIVE

There are some moments in your life that completely take away the person that you might have become.

I was twenty-two years old when THAT MOMENT happened for me. It's a moment that has made me who I am today. It has made me the wife I am today. The mother I am today. It has made me vulnerable. It has made me strong. It has made me resilient. It has made me a survivor.

This is my "A Survivor's Perspective". It was written at 3am on September 11, 2016. I woke up with so many thoughts going through my mind, so I sat up in bed and put them to paper.

I remember each day how I will never be the same....
I remember the massive fireball coming from tower one as I started to walk back to my desk....

GINA CLAPPROOD

I remember hearing a co-worker say "get the hell out of here".... I listened, he saved my life....

I remember wondering what stairwell to go down.... I made the right choice....

I remember walking calmly down 94 flights of stairs....

I remember feeling the building sway when the plane hit tower two......I was below it....

I remember them telling us to "go back to your desks, Two World Trade is in no imminent danger"......I did not listen, this saved my life....

I remember waiting to call my family and hearing a rumble, a police officer saying, "Run! Run!".... this was my building collapsing....

I remember a guy behind me running and almost pushing me down as his hand came down on top of my head....

I remember meeting a girl named Erin and walking with her uptown....

I remember people in Midtown shopping.... they didn't know what happened yet....

I remember finally calling home and hearing my grandmother cry....no one believed it was me....

I remember seeing my friends and not really understanding what was happening but hugging them tightly....

I remember listening to my friend recount what happened to me hours later and finally breaking down....

I remember the years that would follow and never feeling quite "right" and people telling me "you should just be happy you survived"....

I remember waking up from nightmares, my whole body was warm like fire and a smoke sensation filled my mouth....

I remember my first panic attack....

I remember going through awful times....

I remember getting better....

I remember each day looking at my phone or my computer and it tells me it's 9:11....

I remember how the clock in my mom's house stopped working and the hands landed on 9 and 11 and we will not change it....

I remember how I will never be the same in more ways than I can describe....

I remember how I have so many friends and family who think of me on this day and send me love......thank you....

And I remember I am here for a reason. ❤

This year, my dad asked me if I was going to write something about September 11th, similar to what I wrote in 2016. I said, "no, that was a once in a lifetime writing that just seemed to pour from my soul", however I did give this some thought and as I felt this year has been a defining moment for me (maybe it is because I'm 40), I decided to write about my "New Perspective".

One of the many ways that I have been affected by September 11th is how I feel when it comes to traveling by plane. I am not fearful of crashing into a building because that would be crazy, right? Well, in the last 17 years, I've actually only travelled alone, on a plane, three times.

1) In 2008 I flew to Texas when my husband's father passed away. My husband left the day before and although he would be with his

family, I also wanted to be there for him and for them during this difficult time.

2) In May 2018, I was asked to surprise one of my best girls for her 4Oth birthday and I *really* struggled with going because I would need to fly across the country, on my own. But after 18 years I WAS NOT going to let my fear get the best of me and I was going to hug my Jennifer.

3) In August 2018 I went on a business trip and while I flew down to Pittsburgh with my colleague, I had to fly home alone. Surprisingly, this time, I was so calm and didn't give it a second thought. Though my trip was short, I spent the most memorable time with my Karen and I was able to snuggle and see how amazing her son, Andrew, is!

Since September 11, 2001, I always try to be vigilant in my surroundings, but I can't let my fears get the best of me and take away the amazing experiences that life can bring, and I most certainly need to show my children that fear can't hold us back.

So, what did I do to show my children I am not fearful? I went on a few rides at Santa's Village in New Hampshire. Now, do not laugh! One of the rides was a swing ride that went around in a circle, but it felt like I was just going to get tossed right in the air and the second ride was a roller coaster. It didn't go upside down, but it sure went fast enough for me to scream and for my husband to laugh at me.

And lastly, in this 40th year if mine, I have come to appreciate just how short life can be. Cliché, I know – but not as cliché anymore for me. My hope is that I am remembered as someone who was always smiling no matter what life threw at me and that I always made you feel like you mattered.

I am a Selfish B.

7 CORRIE DOUGLAS | I SIMPLIFIED MY LIFE

My Inner Bitch finally came out a year ago. This is when I was finally honest with myself and did something about it.

For years, I was just coasting along professionally. I had these nagging inner thoughts and feelings that I wasn't doing what I was supposed to be doing. But I would talk myself out of those and just continue on like a robot just doing what I was comfortable doing. I feel like for me, as I got older, I really didn't like change anymore and if I was in a situation, I didn't love it was ok because I'd rather sacrifice happiness then deal with change and the unknown.

But as the months and years were fleeting by me, I was really wanting to be my own boss. I have been working since I was 14 years old, I was now in my 40's and I was feeling kind of done with my destiny being in the hands of someone else. Will l I ever get a raise, a promotion, can I take this day off? I was done with having to ask for these things from someone else. I wanted to be independent and control what I make, what I do, when I work. I finally wanted to take control of me. But, the million-dollar question was what can I do?

As my personal life was thrown into chaos when my now husband moved into my cozy little house with all of his life's belongings and we had our son a few months later, which along with this cute little baby, came stuff and lots of it! While probably losing my mind, I started to take my personal space back! I purged, organized and set up systems to store kitchen items, toys, baby items.

I set up systems in closets, pantries, inside of closet doors, empty walls going down to the basement any space I had I utilized it! I loved to organize! I loved the control and sense of calm it instantly brought when things were purged, and organizational systems were put into place.

So, I started to do the same for others just for fun. Friends and family would ask my opinion on how they could organize their space. I realized I could see the potential of a space that other people couldn't visualize for themselves.

I then decided I wanted to become a Professional Organizer. I wanted to help people feel and live in an environment they are happy to be in. I was still working at my job while trying to get the details of my business started. I started building my website, thinking of a business name and logo and trying to come up with a marketing plan.

That's when I left my job of 11 ½ years and ventured out on my own. It took a huge leap of faith and was one of the scariest things to do but I couldn't ignore my inner self anymore. That's when Simplify Your Life was born, and I haven't looked back!

I am a Boss.

8 LOUISE ROSA | REFLECTIONS

YESTERDAY

In the spring of 1979, at the age of 30, I made my first major purchase: A Cape Cod summer home in West Dennis, Massachusetts. The three-bedroom cottage was previously owned by a dear cousin, and its purchase was a perfect rite of passage for me. Not only did the house offer a picturesque atmosphere, with shade trees, colorful flowers, and bird houses, it was a short walk to a beautiful beach. I knew that I could make a summer home and have a lifestyle that would offer me fun with friends and family. This would signal a sense of accomplishment, personal fulfillment, and happiness.

I spent that summer decorating the knotty pine interior with furnishings to make a house a home. What fun I had with my parents at my side helping me choose what I needed to live comfortably in my new retreat. With many friends and family, someone was always available to spend a weekend with me. Some even rented my home for their own fun time!

As the years passed, I became more accustomed to caring for the house and yard, and I found myself enjoying every aspect of ownership, especially yard work! I fondly remember being alone and planting flowers and trimming the lawn and tree branches. These long days spent in my yard always culminated in a luxurious hot shower in the private, enclosed attachment to my home. The aroma of pine and the sound of the rustling trees always invigorated and relaxed me. The shower became a favorite venue for all who visited!

May 25, 1989 marked a horrific event that occurred suddenly and unexpectedly at my vacation home. On that sunny Friday afternoon my beloved father, who always spent time at my cottage, lovingly and masterfully remodeling it, collapsed in the backyard. I remember the painful phone calls and the interminable ride to Cape Cod Hospital. Once there, my sister, brother-in-law, and I met my mother who told us that my father had died. I felt enormous loss: for my father and for the carefree times my cottage represented. It was now a place of sadness.

Over the next month, with the help of family and friends, I began to emerge from the overwhelming sadness. I realized that now I held sole responsibility for care of my summer home. Since the beach has always offered me solace, I became determined to make days spent by the ocean ones that would help me heal. Fun times slowly returned, only to be cut short by the untimely death of my mother, just 10 months after my father's passing. How could I find peaceful refuge once more? I realized that I would need to return to my Cape Cod cottage to regain that peace and to persevere. And so, I did.

Throughout the nineties and the early years of the new millennium, I relished my days in the yard, at the beach, and in my cozy cottage. Once again, I shared many delightful times with friends. Once again, it was a place to enjoy and to celebrate. Two exceptionally memorable events were hosting a family reunion for relatives from Italy and a family week-long farewell to a dear friend dying of cancer. My home was both a site of celebration and solace.

After 25 years, I felt the need to travel beyond the Cape. I wanted to spread my wings. I had a difficult decision to make. Should I keep the cottage or sell it and use the money to travel afar? Would selling it diminish all the fond memories of those years there? Would I relish new experiences with the same enjoyment? How could I let go? How could I leave those memories behind? Fear grasped my mind and caused great angst. Selling would signal another rite of passage.

I sought the advice of friends, in conversations over many cups of coffee or glasses of wine. Gradually, as I understood my needs, I came to a decision: I would sell the cottage. My plan for the next 25 years would be to take care of myself and travel the world, while cherishing the memories and experiences.

TODAY

At times my dreams take me back to the cottage. My mind wanders from struggle and sadness to leisure afternoons reading and napping on the porch, gardening, hosting parties, lolling on the beach, shopping, and dining out at favorite restaurants. These dreams give comfort, for they help me to move forward while appreciating the opportunities I have had and continue to have.

During my years at the Cape, I found great satisfaction sharing my home with family and friends, offering them respite, solace, relaxation, and the real "Cape Cod experience." My travels now lead me to discover new worlds -from Hawaii to Alaska to Italy to Caribbean Islands to Scandinavia and beyond – and a continued renewal and rediscovery of me!

I am a Selfish B.

Louise Rosa. M. Ed. | English Teacher: North Providence High School in North Providence, RI | Communications Professor: Johnson and Wales University in Providence, RI

9 KATHRYN GNIADEK | SAY 'YES' TO WHAT MAY SCARE YOU

In my formative childhood years, I lived with a lot of change and instability which led to many of my insecurities and self-doubt. As to be expected, I carried that into adulthood. Thankfully I still had an underlying strength that would get me through most situations that I was not truly confident about.

As I grew older and had children, my confidence started to emerge more. My main goal as a mother was to raise confident children because I had seen how it could get you places in this world. I knew that in order to have confident children, I had to be a positive role model for them.

At 34 years old, I had three young children at home, no experience running a business and very limited time for myself, but my gut kept pushing me towards doing something with my newfound talent. I had just learned to sew at age 30.

I LOVE working. I like the responsibility, the respect and the paycheck. I love being a mom, which is proving to be one of the most difficult jobs on earth, but I knew I wanted more for myself.

And I knew it would make me a better mom to make time for myself to do something that made me truly happy.

So, I started this small business of making handbags. I have since added jewelry, other accessories and a t-shirt line. I had always been a people pleaser and always felt like I had something to prove. I still struggle with that to this day but much less than I used to.

When I started the business, I would try to please everyone and I made bags with fabrics that I would NEVER use for myself but I felt like I had to get something for everyone so that EVERYONE would love my stuff.....but I have learned through the years that I will never please everyone and not everyone will like my brand and be a customer. I now only make products out of fabrics and jewelry findings that I love, that I would want to wear. And if what I design is not someone's cup of tea then so be it. There is something else out there for them. I have to be true to myself in the end.

My advice to anyone who wants to follow their passion and start their own business is the following…

One - be confident in your abilities and talents.

Two - don't give up even when you face challenges, because you will. If you are certain that this is what you want to do, work through those road bumps and you will come out stronger and more sure when you do.

Three - don't doubt yourself. There will always be people that don't share your same taste or style or thoughts or opinions... If you know it's something of worth and value, there will be others that do as well.

Four - don't rush the process… I did this so many times in the beginning. I was so excited for a new product that I didn't want to wait until I perfected it and I would put something less than stellar out for the consumer and it was a waste because it wasn't what it should have been if I had just taken the time…. You know what they say, haste makes waste!

Five - talk to as many people as possible. Talk to people in your field, people that would be your target customer, bloggers in your niche and google everything. The more information and knowledge you have the better.

And last but not least, say YES to things that may scare you. If there are opportunities that are out of your comfort zone but may benefit you in the long run, say yes.

I have worked really hard to get where I am but have so much further to go. But the progress I've made in myself so far makes me hopeful for the future and how much more I can accomplish. Some of my confidence still lays dormant but when it emerges, the things I will accomplish! So, keep your eyes out for me.

I AM A BOSS!

10 KAREN SPENCER | TELL YOURSELF YOU ARE A BADASS!

When asked to contribute to Gina's third book, I was honored and honestly it took me a few months to figure out which way I wanted to go with this. I feel like there have been so many defining moments in my journey on this earth thus far. It is hard to think of one single moment that has taught me how to be myself.

I've always tried to honor being myself in every situation even as a young girl. I guess I've always been a "call it as I see it kind of person". Fakeness or conformity make my skin crawl. I gravitate to authentic people. I'm interested in being my authentic self in every relationship and when that isn't possible, I'm not interested.

Being the youngest of seven kids makes you resilient, I guess. I've seen many struggles in my family over the years but all of them and the experiences have molded me in the person I am today. I've watched my Mom handle the impossible and never shy away from the struggle. This has always spoken to me and my inner voice is one tough cookie because of it. I approach most situations with confidence because I have watched my parents handle some real tough situations and love each other through all of them. They never gave up on each other and remained madly in love all these years.

It was 2004 when I first heard about Girls On The Run (GOTR). A friend gave me the book "Girls on Track." written by GOTR founder Molly Barker. My friend's daughter was struggling a little bit socially in the 4th grade. Some of her friends were telling her she couldn't do a cartwheel, so she couldn't play with them at recess. I said to my friend's daughter, "You know what I would do? I'd stand there and do my horrible cartwheels at recess right next to those girls." She just looked at me and said, "I could never do that". About a month after that conversation my friend slid me the book across the table while we were sharing a cup of coffee. Her sister had sent her the book from California. My friend said, "YOU need to do this program with our girls, YOU could do this, YOU were made to teach this program!"

Well after a few more babies and some family challenges along the way, Girls on the Run kept coming up in my life. Every time I would put it on the back burner it would somehow bubble up to the surface and give me a little nudge.

In 2014 I finally got the courage to take the plunge. During the process of the monstrous GOTR application – which totaled 297 pages. As proposed Council Director, I was asked to answer the question "Why are you interested in starting a council of Girls on the Run?" WOW! Why did I want to REALLY start a council so badly?

I've reflected back on my life and all the reasons for wanting to start this council. I have had several friends over the years say to me "you are the most confident person I have ever met" and when I think back on my life and try to find the reasons why that may be true, I always come back to what I learned about myself through sports.

When I was a freshman in high school, I tried out for the field hockey team and I remember seeing this older girl, a fiery red head named Susan, she was so amazing, and she had this confidence on and off the field that I had never seen before. It wasn't until my sophomore year that I became close friends with Sue. Through that friendship Susan reminded me how to celebrate my strengths and abilities and never downplay my talents. I learned from Susan to embrace my competitive edge and to never be afraid to be strong and true to myself.

When I started dating my now husband, Don, the summer going in to our Junior year of high school, we challenged each other in every sport imaginable. Do you know how hard it is to play field hockey one on one? If I had to play another game of RISK one more time, I might have strangled myself. Don never let me off the hook, he still doesn't, he challenges me and never lets me win. Don inspires me to be my best and give my best 100% of the time.

When I look back, turns out I had a really hard year in 2002 – my sister passed away in February from years of substance abuse and my friend Susan (that fiery red head) passed away of ovarian cancer in August that same year. I really struggled with these two deaths. I struggled with the two very different extremes of self-worth. I remember thinking what are you going to do to make a difference? Did I want to do something to help people with substance abuse? One of my professors in college said try to be "proactive" in business… I thought to myself: Why not be proactive in LIFE?!

I may not be able to change what happened to my sister but how could I be "proactive" enough to try to prevent substance abuse in young girls before it even starts? How do you "teach" someone how to love herself? How do you "teach" them confidence? How do you teach them they are WORTHY? How do you reach girls BEFORE they develop a self-esteem issue?

GIRLS ON THE RUN is how you REACH those girls…

I'll close with a little story, our daughter is a competitive swimmer, she has been since the age of 7 1/2. When she started competing she would get these belly aches right before her heat, like clockwork we would head to the bathroom… one particular swim meet the conversation went something like "do you get a little nervous before you are getting ready to race?" and she said – I remember it like it was yesterday… "yes mom, but once I get up on those starting blocks, it all goes away mom and I feel great" This from a seven and a half year old - can you believe it? I knew then, that we were doing something right.

I remember a time in college, studying Architecture and felt very miscast, my professor use to give us a project to complete by the next class and everyone would have to present their project to the class. I would always volunteer to go first. I hated waiting there while others presented. I'd rather go first and get it over with. This one particular day, my professor graded me harshly and gave me a 'C', I took my lumps and sat down. After several classmates presented, he realized that he wasn't clear in the assignment. He interrupted one student and said "Karen, give yourself a 'B' instead, mark down that I gave you a 'B'". I replied "no, I don't think so". He replied, "excuse me?" I said, "You gave me a 'C' and that is what I'll take". He later gave me an 'A' on the assignment.

After studying Architecture for a couple of years, I decided to transfer to a Business school. I remember a situation where we had a group project and one of my partners had got his section all wrong. When I told him, he refused to believe it, so I said let's go find the professor and you can tell him. So many times, people ignore their inner voice and don't speak up for themselves for fear of being called a bitch. Why not honor yourself and forget about hurting someone else's feelings?

In 2011, out of nowhere I started having panic attacks. It was a time that some extended family issues were going on and I wasn't being true to my own feelings and putting others ahead of myself and my immediate family. In retrospect, if I had stayed true to my own truth, I would have battled the panic attacks much sooner than I did. I tried medication and had a severe allergic reaction. I reached out to a meditative healer who brought me through a peaceful meditation exercise that helped me hear my inner voice. I still practice this when I start to feel a little anxious.

I take time for myself often. I also encourage my husband to do the same. I know that he loves to coach, he comes alive when he is coaching. So, I try to support him in every way I can, so he can carve out time to devote. It is important to do the things that bring you joy and to support others to do the same. I love to go to CrossFit, it is my time to work hard physically and connect with friends. It is the closest thing I have found that replicates playing sports in high school and college. CrossFit helps me work on strengthening my mental game and reminds me I can do anything I put my mind to.

In closing, my advice to others would be to honor your own truth, trust your instincts and believe in yourself and tell yourself you are a "BADASS" and can take on anything you put your mind to. **I am a BADASS.**

11 MARIA MARILYN PORRECA |
OVER THE GRATES IN HEELS

A Chapter by Maria Marilyn Porreca

"There is a sacredness in tears. They are not the mark of weakness, but of power. They speak more eloquently than ten thousand tongues. They are the messengers of overwhelming grief, of deep contrition, and of unspeakable love." - *Washington Irving*

When Gina asked me to participate in her new book by contributing a chapter, I was incredibly honored. I began the process of reflecting on 40 years and outlining and summarizing the challenges and lessons in my life up to this point. For each challenge and lesson, I have a story of success because I listened and learned (I am here! :)). I have learned that the more open I am to a new challenge results in a road that accelerates my personal journey. The key to it all is knowing your core value system, maintaining high standards and finding comfort and patience within yourself to understand that we are here to learn and practice our values over time. No one is perfect, everyone is perfect.

This is not a comprehensive story, but instead I did my best to highlight experiences on my path that I found most challenging and how I benefitted from the lessons. The order of this chapter is based on the lessons learned which are not always aligned with the timing of the experience that led me there. I hope that anyone reading this chapter finds a piece of themselves that we share or perhaps my lessons will also become your success stories.

An Overview of Me

It is 2018 and I am 40 years old. I live in the borough of Manhattan in New York City and I practice finance at a well-known, global organization. I am healthy, happy and more than self-sufficient with a road of growth and experiences ahead that excite me. I know that any day can bring challenges, but I am healthy and strong enough to carry the uncertainty of life. I love to read, share with and learn from others. I am blessed with family love and full of gratitude. I wake-up every day with a smile, thankful when my feet touch the ground with anticipation to walk another day, filled with energy to learn. My parents instilled incredible work ethics within me. I am happily married, we are preparing for our twin girls to arrive in early 2019. We have a sweet shih tzu named A.J. that I adopted from Animal Haven. We recently lost my other precious shih tzu, Ivy, who I adopted from Bideawee.

A Bit of 'Herstory'

Seventeen plus years ago, I moved to Manhattan and the experiences continue to be rich with incredible opportunity to learn and grow as a citizen of the world that I continue to seek. Some of the experiences were more of a challenge than immediate joy and how I came to this point is a direct correlation of where I started. The core of the person I am started in my hometown of North Providence, RI and every piece of my life is who I am today. I love every moment of witnessing the world through my eyes and I am always excited to have the opportunity to look though someone else's lens...you never know what you may learn and collectively the experiences are so much richer.

Our experiences over time differ and shape how we manage ourselves, others and the opinions and perceptions we form. Basically, our exposure forms the characters we ultimately become. The experiences are attached to where we live, the culture we practice, the books we read, the people that surround us, how often and where we travel, etc.… The more exposure we have, the more well-rounded and thoughtful we are in our choices and opinions because we have more facts from a larger selection of experiences to support our decisions and beliefs which increases our confidence level. The more we are open to new challenges, expected or spontaneous, the more we really learn about ourselves. The more we are open to the journey of learning, the more happiness we will find within ourselves.

My Value System is Born

Everyone's anchor in life is different. For me, my family has always been my anchor. I understand that everyone's definition of family differs. For me, my parents and my brother were my key support for the first half of my life. *If I close my eyes and go back to my childhood home, it is rich with love and happiness. A very*

close family where attendance at the dinner table is mandatory and
we share our daily experiences and questions. The open dialogue

at our table is where we learned to be open to trust and share

anything from our lightest to our deepest thoughts and to challenge

those thoughts. It is these moments that formed the solid

foundation which kept our bonds strong. That mandatory time

together was an easy fulfillment as my mom poured love into

every meal and the delicious flavor was a symbol of the time, she

spent perfecting healthy, delicious meals for her family and many

frequent guests. When I think of my childhood, I can taste the love

and it fills me with so much warmth. Our home was always filled

with family and friends as it was so easy to be attracted to my

parents because they shined with love and their warm rays reached

all who entered. In our home, everyone felt like they were a part of

our family. There was always music playing with laughter and the

chatter of happy voices. My childhood experiences formed my

core values and it is these values that I always return to and lean on

in times of difficulty. I am forever grateful for the unselfish time

and energy my parents gave to us. They both worked full-time at

their jewelry business and their incredible work ethic and family values truly shaped who I am and the opportunities I have made for my adult self. I realize the gift of their time is everything that has made the difference in my life. And I realize that the value of time is priceless because it is so limited. To this day, my parents are my greatest mentors and I still go to them for advice when I am perplexed. My brother has since passed, but the lessons he left me whether through our many talks together or by witnessing his life are still very relevant to this day to which I am very grateful.

Dealing with his loss was my greatest lesson to date and that lesson created a reality of what a "bad day" really is...and my perception was strengthened as a result. I will touch on examples in this chapter.

The Beginning of Change

When I was 17 years old, I went to Syracuse University (SU). This was a very exciting time of my life and I will truly always cherish those years as a young adult with my first experience of independence from my family home. From the application process, college campus visits/tours to the letter of acceptance…I enjoyed every moment and we were all so excited. I remember my parents, brother and his girlfriend (who was like an older sister) brought me to Syracuse and helped me decorate my dorm room. I was very excited for this new experience and they were very hesitant to leave me…the memories of that time fill me with joy. If I could take those days back, I would hold them so tight because as I was starting my journey as a young adult towards independence, my brother was taking a path that was leading him to horrific dependence and a connection to a new set of people that would make his life increasingly difficult. If I think back to the summer that I left for college, there were subtle clues of new people that he brought to our home and his girlfriend raised a concern to our family. I was 17 and he was 25.

Learning the importance of maintaining my value system:
Lesson 1

The happy family that departed Syracuse University was soon facing a drug addiction and my brother's uncharacteristic life choices. By the second semester of my freshman year at SU my brother and his girlfriend separated, and my brother suddenly eloped. I will never forget when my mother called me at college to share the news…she said she thought it was a joke at first because it was so unbelievable and then when she realized it was true she felt like she had been punched in the stomach. This reality became ours so quickly…my brother was snorting heroin, and this was the beginning of a brutal addiction and a path that ultimately would lead to his walk to heaven. Less than four years later at my college graduation, as I was walking the stage to accept degrees in both International Relations and Women's' Studies, my parents were dealing with a call from the neighbor that my brother and another person were on the front lawn of our family home high on drugs.

The fact that he was not at the graduation with my parents was evidence enough that he was not in a healthy state. He was gifted, intelligent, handsome, incredibly active and excelled at every sport, but like rats and cockroaches, this disease does not discriminate, and it had a hold on him. Our lives were completely altered, and our happy, healthy home was now filled with the darkness of drug addiction. The family values to which we were so accustomed were a struggle for him to practice at that time. The holiday tables that were once filled with people and voracious appetites that were satisfied with the homemade food my mother served was now often left with filled plates as we now dealt with the drug withdrawals. The laughter and family discussions were left behind as my family and I tried to learn how to take each next step and deal with a disease that we knew nothing about...We honestly tried, but, like any disease, drug addiction is a reality of what it really means to live life day by day with hope for a better day. I still do not know how my parents coped...living every unpredictable day dealing with trying to find a solution to combat this brutal disease. Everyone suffers, but in the short-run the pain is excruciating for the sober family that has no control and only prayer. The time is filled with trial-and-error solutions that are long and exhausting. I certainly pray every day for science to win this war and succeed in the battle to combat addiction.

After college graduation, I returned home for one-year and one-half for family reasons. First, to build a bond with my God-son/nephew who was born when I was studying abroad in France and Italy during my junior-year of college. Second, my paternal grandfather was diagnosed with cancer and my grandparents moved into our family home. I was very close to my grandfather and tried to spend as much time with him as I could watching movies and sharing stories. In typical form, my father and mother were amazing at this time, but I felt I needed to be there to help them manage the constant waves of visits from family and friends from the U.S and Italy and to spend time with my grandfather before he passed. I quickly took a job as a waitress and began looking for jobs and researching Peace Corp opportunities and Master's and JD Programs. I had a few options that I was excited about, but my mom thought I should take it slow in my "quest to save the world", learn how to take care of myself and consider a role in finance. Approximately six months later, she backed up her case with a job ad circled for me in the newspaper and shortly after applying I went to work for a new company in RI called Suretrade.com as a broker trainee. And so, it began that I had now kicked-off my career in finance. I did not realize at this time, but my decision to move home would have a bigger impact than I imagined.

Shortly after my grandfather passed away, my brother and his wife divorced, and his ex-wife moved approximately 1-hour+ away to a nearby state. This new chapter meant my brother had a fighting chance. He moved back to my parent's home, continued working and my parents and I supported his process of rehabilitation and recovery. Each morning, either my father or I drove him to work.

Ultimately, he kicked heroin and started to get his spirit back and his energy for life returned. As my brother's health improved, he became active again in education opportunities and physical fitness. Most of all, he focused on his greatest joy which was being a father. He and my nephew played sports, enjoyed movies, he often read Harry Potter to my nephew, practiced math problems in workbooks with my nephew and encouraged education and sports. I remember them getting ready together in the bathroom mirror as my brother taught his son to brush his teeth, carefully choose his attire and how to do his hair…they both took great pride in their style. They were adorable together. My nephew was with us quite often spending every weekend and the school holidays. Those days with my brother were wonderful…we went back to enjoying quality time together as a family for some years.

The impact that my brother's life had on mine was profound…his challenges gave me insight to make better decisions in my own life. I cannot talk about myself without including my brother's experiences as they gave me direction that I otherwise may not have had the opportunity to learn from at such an early part of my own life.

I learned an important lesson from my brother during that time. This experience lived with me as there were many difficult days for my brother, but he always chose to see the bigger picture and focus on my nephew. I would continue to learn this after my brother died…his actions guided me. Values are important, and he managed and was able to forgive others, love and maintain his focus on his son. His values remained at a high standard despite the challenges that were presented to him. His actions of love for his family allowed him to supersede any unnecessary drama. My brother was a critical part in my patient selection of a husband

and father. I spent more time seeking a man that would be a great father as it was the most important qualification to me. I now look forward to spending time with my family, reading Harry Potter and practicing math with my daughters and teaching them the importance of core values and high standards with my husband.

Confidence & Character

When I was 18, I knew that I wanted to be confident, but it took more than 15 years to attach a word to describe the presence that I witnessed and wanted to become, and I continue to practice every day by studying, reading and exposing myself to new and different experiences. The way I remember this feeling I had was through the presence of a woman I met though my college internship in Providence, RI. I did not know her name or meet her formally. We were at an event and she had a quality that I was not yet able to describe…she filled the room with a peaceful strength that I could sense, and I knew I wanted to emulate that characteristic. I thought she was humble, but it was confidence. I now realize that what we sometimes perceive as humble is really confidence. She had enough knowledge to know where she was and who she was, and she was comfortable to share and learn, but she had nothing to prove to anyone. She was comfortable and secure in her own, imperfect skin.

Another recollection is at the age of 19 years old, at that time I could not wait to be 30 years old because I envisioned this decade as a time when one's feet were firmly rooted in the ground and life was figured out and in place. To be honest, 30 seemed very far away at 19 years old…LOL What I perceived as a level of confidence was actually 11 years of experiences that I did not yet have as I was just trying to figure out answers to my 19-year old questions that I did not have at the tip of my tongue quite yet…actually, often times I was trying to figure out the right questions to ask. Ultimately, my life proved to be quite a different experience as 29 – 34 years old were the most challenging lessons of my life to date. I often refer to that time in my life as the years of "Whiplash". It is in these years that I learned first-hand to deal with what I cannot control and loss.

Next Stop Manhattan and the Virtue of Patience: Lesson 2

My time back at home in RI and working at Suretrade.com was an incredible experience. I built the foundation for a wonderful relationship with my Godson/nephew and spent valuable time with my family. However, it was time for me to move on and pursue my path. After all, my parents always supported building my wings to fly…and so I came home one-day and let my mom know I was moving to NY. The next day I received a call from Morgan Stanley and based on that call I was offered an in-person job interview and subsequently hired after my interview the next week. I found my own apartment for $900 per month. A couple of weeks later I moved to White Plains and on August 1, 2001, I started my new job as a Financial Advisor. My parents and boyfriend at the time helped me move in…the place was decent, but it had recently been upgraded and the place was a mess, so we had to clean it, but once it was decorated and my own – it was perfect. In hindsight, I would have moved in with roommates. I did not realize then that I could have had a roommate or two in NYC for the same price (it was and still is expensive for a young college grad just starting out).

I love NYC and I have loved it from the first time I arrived. The energy suited me…and I worked my butt off and took in all the experiences I could. I began to meet many people and build my life. I also waitressed in the evenings at a NYC restaurant for one-month+ to raise more money to support my independence. I did what I could and enjoyed every moment. Eventually I found another job at an insurance brokerage, thickened my skin and built what would eventually become the financial planning and analysis department. I had a blast analyzing that portfolio, building reports for executives, telling the stories of numbers, financials statements, valuations, proformas and databases were my joy. My technical skills were on fire. I worked day and night…and lived every moment enjoying the bright lights of the Big Apple late-night. I only required 4 hours of uninterrupted sleep and I maximized that time to the fullest. The stories are certainly grand, and I had so much fun building my life here, traveling the U.S and abroad and making incredible friends.

From the Financial District to Harlem (and a few times Brooklyn)…I experienced 9/11, the NYC Black-Out, Hurricane

Sandy, Washington Square Park (my fav!), Fashion Week shows and parties, World Series, Box Seats and Suites, NYC Halloween Parades, The Mermaid Parade and many more, NYC Marathons, Greenwich Village, Central Park, Westside Highway, Sutton Place Parks, Elaine's, Brio, The Four Seasons Restaurant, L&B's Spumoni Garden, Felice and just the daily grind of making it in the big city. This city is beautiful, and I was fortunate enough to experience the finest of all of it! I have so much respect for the people of NYC. They are resilient and never short of lending a helping hand to those in need. This is a city built on philanthropy. A city where poor, wealthy, middle-class and the most diverse crowds sit together to eat, drink and share stories about life. This city was everything I craved, and I was and continue to be so happy to be here. Duffy aka Kevin from Elaine's will tell you that my eyes were bigger than my head as I did everything I could to absorb it all…at just 23 years old.

I lived with my boyfriend for a while and then he proposed. He was an incredible man and so close to my family. I was 26 when he proposed marriage and my career was starting…we were so young and eventually I had to let that relationship go. He was wonderful, but my gut told me that it would not last past 30 years old...and so I made the difficult decision to return the ring and move on. It was hard for us and our families. Our parents were devastated because we all really loved each other so much. In the end it worked out to be as God intended and he is married to a wonderful woman and I am married to a wonderful man.

Women, including myself, are often still questioned about their choices to wait to marry and/or have children. This can be annoying. There is still an incredible pressure on the "clock count-down", but honestly there are many options for women today and this pressure to create insecurity in women's fertility or to remain unmarried and happy and free to be patient is unnecessary. I chose to wait to have children and focus on my career. When I was 37, I chose to freeze my eggs and gifted myself those golden eggs on my 38th birthday (I was blessed by the Pope 3x that week on East 65th Street in NYC...LOL). This action gave me options to have my own children if I did not find a suitable partner for parenting or have a back-up plan if I experienced fertility issues or simply choose to take a more aggressive approach. Today, many young women have options and frankly I recommend exploring fertility options as early as possible if a woman is interested in pursuing a career. There is no right or wrong order to having children – age is just a number. For me, I wanted to secure my financial health to better care for my future children. My brother died at an early age and because of that I wanted to have a plan to offer them a financially secure life. I never had any insecurities about my fertility because I knew I was healthy based on fertility blood tests. That means, I was confident that menopause and known infertility risks were not yet a concern, and I had facts to maintain my confidence in my plans. Time was on my side despite any myths. I am fully-accountable, and it is critical that I am always involved in decisions and risk options when it comes to the financial security of myself and my family. For young women considering a career, explore your options early and celebrate the right to have patience and make good decisions for yourself in the order you choose. You have options. Life is a miracle and there are no guarantees at any age. If you learn that fertility is not an option, I recommend that you consider adoption. Love is what it this all about. Follow your path and have a plan. Afterall, the gift of motherhood is much more than giving birth…it is about the love and support you provide as a parent which most valued.

Choices in Good Company and Boundaries: Lesson 3

The Company You Keep

The "raccoon" stole my credit reputation temporarily, a bit of my heart for a short time and basically lived off me financially and even had the audacity to take girls on dates using my credit card (or at least one every expensive date). He even guilted me into another credit card that he maxed when he experienced a family loss which helped to support his summer in a popular New England summer destination. Initially, I believed he was building his business for our life together, but instead I paid for too many golf trips, his friends showers and weddings, dates with girls and nights out drinking, etc. I let this go on for too long because I thought I really loved him. The reality is that I was not paying enough attention because I was so busy building my own career and towards the very end of the relationship I was dealing with the loss of my brother. But like any good analyst, I found all the evidence, made a conclusion and shipped him out. But it still hurt immensely at that time. I went home to RI on Labor Day and woke my mother up early in the morning and asked her to stay with me for 3 weeks to make sure he did not try to move back in after the summer. My father drove us back to NYC that day. It worked.

That relationship cost me more than tears and really taught me about securing my finances and credit reputation. I had a lot of work to do to get myself out of that financial mess that I allowed wearing those rose-colored glasses…At the time, I worked intense days, including weekends, averaging 15-18 hours so a 2nd job was not really an option. I was literally living paycheck to paycheck to pay and settle the debts and timing was everything to survive each week during this time. He agreed to pay me monthly, but he refused to sign an agreement and he defaulted almost immediately. I held my own overall, but I remember when I did not have the money for Christmas presents for my nephew because I was now struggling to make ends meet during that time and supporting myself in Manhattan. My parents let me borrow the money and

Christmas was saved. My parents have truly been my anchor so many times…God bless them.

Reputation is so important…especially in the credit markets. I learned a hard lesson and had many nights to reflect on it while I ate cereal or cheese and olives over my kitchen sink. I basically always had my own general ledger of accounts and managed my cash flow quite well, but I learned a hard lesson the moment I turned my head and stopped paying attention and prioritizing my life for others. It took years for me to recover, but I did recover in time. It is so important to keep your finances in order and if you are going to loan out your credit reputation for another, make sure you have a contract in place or be prepared to sue in court or treat it as a loss and move on…

Healthy Boundaries and Loyalty

I elected to go to therapy a few times in my life as I am a firm believer in working thorough my feelings and I work hard not to repress what I know will eventually show itself. I also went to a church bereavement group after the loss of my brother which was incredibly helpful. In my early 30's, I spent 2 years of therapy working to understand that loyalty to myself and being my own best friend need to come first. It is never wise to turn your back on yourself in times of disappointment. That is actually when you need yourself the most...I remember sitting in therapy and realizing it was the first time in so long that I was truly focused on myself. That was a critical turning point for me and how I started to develop healthy boundaries for myself. I am a giver and it brings me great joy to contribute to the well-being of community, individuals and animals, but I had to learn how far I could stretch myself without losing sight of my own health and to beware of anyone who expected my health to be less of a priority.

I changed how I was allocating my time and energy on people. My circle of friends became tighter than ever and I appreciated acquaintances with limitations. My health became a priority.

The best advice I ever received was *to always remember that I am in the room.* As a giver I tend to place emphasis on the needs of others to a point that supersedes my own. Realizing this trait and recognizing and knowing myself enough to pull back when I am allowing it at the expense of my well-being is my own checks and balances to remain healthy. Remember, I spent 2 years in therapy to correct this trait and when I started therapy I realized it was the only hour of the week when I truly focused on myself…and overtime I graduated and I now self-manage because I know my weaknesses and I have the confidence to know when to push forward and when to pull-back. I learned that I am my own best friend and what that really means to my well-being. I learned that while I am not perfect, I should never be angry with myself…because if I turn my back on myself than I will not have the spirit to pick myself up to learn and grow. Only I have the strength to pick myself up and only I can self-correct and self-manage. In moments of disappointment, anger at myself serves no purpose. The best use of my time is spent finding solutions and learning to execute and grow to be a better version of me. The core of who I am has never changed, but how I manage life, knowing what I can control and cannot control is a valuable skill. Eventually, I adopted a dog named A.J. that filled my life with so much joy…and then with no intentions I met Ivy one-year later. She was a senior dog with health complications and rescued from a kill shelter. Eventually she came home. A.J. and Ivy gave me so much and still do…I could give all day and their love and appreciation is infinite.

All in all, I learned to appreciate myself and the value of time and energy I deliver to be the best I can be every day. I grew up in an environment with so much trust that when I took the experience outside of our home, I was naive and had to learn that relationships should be earned. I thought everyone was like my parents and brother. It took me time to learn and understand that some people lie and can be selfish, manipulative and deceitful. After therapy, I removed rose-colored glasses and looked at people based on their character and actions. I built relationships over time and managed unhealthy relationships. One relationship, a person I met though my brother, was set with a timeline for termination which I was finally able to execute. Sometimes we must breathe deeply and have patience until the time is right for a greater good.

Our core circles are so valuable to our well-being and not everyone should receive an invite to the dinner table. Invitations should be earned, appreciated and valued.

I allowed myself time to heal and look within myself to build a plan for the next chapter. This was my rainbow after all and the pot of gold lessons I received with was worth every growing pain. I had and still have so much ahead of me and I was gifted wisdom early to accelerate my path to the next adventures.

My Lover, My Best Friend and Partner: My Husband

After a few attempts and a month of writing, I agreed to a date in February 2014. It was a Tuesday night at 9:00 PM EST. I went straight from the office. I am so happy that I was never quick to rush to marry or insecure about being single because I can honestly say that by the time, I met my husband I truly appreciated the person he was…his core and my core matched and I knew this on the first date. In other words, our value systems were aligned. It took some serious trial and error and the kissing some rogue frogs before I found my sweet gem. He found me years before and waited patiently. Perhaps he knew…I don't know, but the wait was worth the reward in love tokens for sure. In August 2015, he proposed marriage in Fatima, Portugal...there was no hesitation as he and I were home in our hearts. We married in Manhattan, NY USA (civil) and Venice, Italy (completed our sacrament of marriage) in 2016.

While my friends were getting married and having babies, I never felt I was missing anything. I was so happy for them and celebrated every moment to the fullest. I was content in my life and it took a little time for me to adjust from my single-woman apartment on East 64th Street to co-habitation after marriage. But like all good things, everything fell into place when the time was right. Like my husband says, when you meet the right person you really understand why everyone else before was wrong for you. And he and I are enjoying every challenge and accomplishment in our journey together.

Life Is Our Greatest Asset: Protect and Secure It

In late October of 2006 my brother telephoned, and we discussed his current situation with tears and he was ready to get away and move with me for a while to get his life back in order and determine a plan of action. He was at his girlfriend's home and bringing the garbage out when he telephoned. He was addicted to prescription drugs and after a rehab attempt the previous summer, he was not able to control the disease. What he expressed has lived with me to this day, he advised that prescription drugs were not street drugs and this addiction was much different and he felt perhaps it would be almost impossible "to kick" or control. This was coming from the same person who "kicked" heroin. The consistency of the prescription drugs were different and would not let go…and the withdrawal was painful. We talked for a bit and planned for him to travel home on weekends to visit his son as not to miss regular visits. His son was always his greatest concern and together we would do anything to make sure our family was well taken care of to the best of our ability.

On November 6th he was supposed to come to NYC with me. I was in RI and would return to NYC that day. He had an obligation that week and he said he could not leave and asked me to understand that we would need to delay his temporary move to NYC with me.

My brother passed away at the age of 36 years. He was in a terrible car accident at approximately 6:00 AM EST, November 10, 2006. He crashed into a pole in RI. The destruction to the vehicle was astounding…the car was completely smashed. When the cops arrived at the scene, they took my brother directly to the police station for a suspended license. To this day there is no paperwork that could be found where my brother signed-off to not go to the hospital which would have been the protocol and by the looks of the vehicle it is exactly where he should have been taken immediately. And the video tapes that the internal police investigator told me they had were "lost" or not available a few days later. My brother was locked in a cell overnight for greater than 24 hours and died there for a suspended license. There was no phone call to my parents. This is all suspect because typically he would have been presented to a judge for a suspended license and released the same day. By the time my parents were notified, by his girlfriend, they rushed to the medical examiner's office where my brothers dead body laid now over 24 hours after he was taken to the police station. They were not allowed to see/claim my brother and the office threatened to call the police if my parents did not leave. To this day I am not sure if my brother died on

November 10th or 11th, but he was pronounced dead on November

11th. Rumor has it that he was seen dead in the jail cell with his

stomach bloated and hanging to the side. His body was cut so

badly by the medical examiner that we had to have a closed casket

service. We opened the casket for immediate family for

approximately 10 minutes before the public service to pay our

respects and lay him with roses. The solution would begin to leak

soon because of how badly they cut and destroyed my brother's

body. The Funeral Director said he had never seen anything like

this in his 40 years of practice.

It was not only the loss of my brother that hurt, but also the pain

and loss of my parents. Much of their spirit went with him that

day. My parents deserved so much more, and this was very

difficult for me to see their spirits broken.

It did not end there, when the medical examiner's report was

issued, they concluded that his death was a result of a drug

overdose. As I mentioned earlier, my brother had a history of drug

use and he was addicted to prescription drugs at this time. His reputation was used against him in what was a case of possible brutality and certainly negligence. I sent the Medical Examiner's report to Suffolk County Medical examiner in NY. I had a contact who was a doctor and she did this as a favor for me. The conclusion in the report did not equate to any medical sense.

According to the reviewer of the medical report, if my brother was on drugs at the time of the accident he would have overdosed immediately or shortly after...not 24+ hours later. That said, by linking a drug overdose to his death the police department was able to fight negligence and the department could use my brother's reputation against him in court...if it went to court.

Dignity, Power-of-Attorney, Executor, Trusts and Family Planning: Lesson 4

The lesson in this story is not about general police actions. I have had many positive experiences with police in both RI and NYC and I do not want to confuse the message of my brother's story. Moreover, on the day of my brother's services there were so many people in attendance that the highways were briefly closed to manage the traffic from the funeral home and we were police

escorted.

That said, I do not believe that the incident was handled properly

by the police officers that were at the scene of the accident the

morning of November 10th. The real lesson to this story is really in

the fact that we were never able to proceed with a case for justice

at all.

Within a few days after my brother's passing, amid planning his

services, managing family visits and dealing with the police

station. I was able to secure a legal team to take my brother's case.

This team was recognized as the best in RI. We were prepared to

move forward and fight both a civil and criminal case, but

honestly, we knew, and the lawyers advised that the drug overdose

report would make the case much more difficult. I just wanted to

maintain my brother's dignity. He was an exceptional person.

Regardless of my brother's reputation with drugs, he did not

deserve to die and have the police negligence swept under the rug.

If he had been taken to a hospital for medical care after the car accident, he may have had the chance to live or at least his body would not have been ripped to pieces during the medical exam. There was one catch, my brother's next of kin was his 9-year old son (a minor) and my brother did not have an estate plan in place to manage his affairs in the event of his death. My parents and I had no rights to my brother's dead body, and we were not able to proceed.

I am not sure of what resulted, but the case was never followed-though with as far as I know, and an independent autopsy was never performed. I could not fight for my brother's dignity. And my parents had no right to their son. Our mistake was that my brother did not have a will and we never thought to have either my parents or I named as power-of attorney while living or executor in the event of his death.

This is a very important lesson. People always think they need assets worth millions to require a living will or estate plans. Our lives are our greatest assets of all – protect and secure your life above anything. It is critical to ensure that there is a plan we trust for all decisions that are required when we are not capable. It is important to have your affairs in order and defined. In life the only thing I know to be consistent is change. That said, make sure your benefits, savings, insurance and living-will and power-of attorney and estate plan are up-to-date and have an annual appointment to review.

Concluding Thoughts

I hope that the reader benefits from the lessons in my life. 40 years is certainly too much to cover in a chapter, but I tried my best to highlight the key lessons.

We all have our lessons, for some they come at childhood and for others much later in life or sometime in between. For me, the major lessons in my life began in college and continued through my mid-30's. I felt confident by 35 years old…and my focus on my health has been a critical part in my decisions since that enlightenment. When my brother passed, it was sort of an existential crisis…I was not the kid sister with a big brother to protect her anymore. He created my crown and made me Super-Woman when I was 6 years old. I now had to learn to place my own crown on my head and become the Queen of my own well-being. My place in life shifted and I had more to learn about myself...and I did. I often think that he and I would have been great business partners...his creative ideas, ability to identify opportunities and my analytic abilities and organization skills. Together, with our stomachs for risk, I believe we would have had an incredible portfolio... We shared so many great times and I celebrate the memories whenever I have the opportunity.

That said, there are so many families that suffer from the disease of addiction. We need to bring attention and not feel ashamed to share our stories because too many great people are dying, if not directly from the disease, then indirectly from the path they are on...and it happens so quickly. One day we are laughing together and very soon after we are preparing to pack the closet. The absorption of the struggles the disease brings is incredible to bear and still is ridden with too many unknowns. There is so much more to learn, and change will come.

If I reflect on the last 40 years, most of my life was filled with happiness and joy – and I had a ton of fun -, but there were some years, particularly between 29 – 34, that I shed tears almost every morning for many different reasons – the challenges I had to work through and process were difficult, but I did not let them hold me down. I listened to a ton of Beyoncé, Lauren Hill, Sam Cooke and others to work through my emotions. Music is a form of therapy for me. There is a song that Sam Cooke sings that I LOVE called 'A Change is Gonna Come'. I had faith in those words, I leaned on my parents and select friends when I was not feeling strong enough and I woke up every day prepared to believe in me and I healed. Every day is a new day and I am so blessed when my feet hit that floor…

We all have our stories…I have shared a bit of mine. There are many aspects of my life that I did not touch on here, such as my dad's prostate cancer and recovery experience which resulted in an amazing time for us together in NYC and RI, climbing the ranks as a woman in finance, etc. I try to reflect and learn from everything. I am not perfect, but I try my best every day and that is all I can do.

I definitely "run hard" to maximize, but I try my best to balance my time and slow down when it is important. That said, I am always working on making more quality time for friends and family without interruption. I work hard, but I know I need to build more relationships outside of the office. I have so many more goals that I would like to achieve, and I feel like I only just started…young at heart I guess because my appetite to learn is still voracious.

Below is a summary of the lessons I have learned and that have become much of who I am and practice:

- I have the confidence to share and the confidence to ask when I am unsure…and I am comfortable knowing that there are no guarantees. That comfort allows me to appreciate my blessings and be grateful for each day.
- I realize that I will keep learning until my time on this earth expires and it brings me immense comfort. After all, if I knew everything what would be my purpose here? …
- I believe that collectively we are stronger together and we can learn from our differences.
- I am a mentor and a mentee.
- I create healthy boundaries.

- I am self-aware.
- I know when to let go and take time to heal.
- I take an honest look at myself in the mirror every day.
- I reflect and take time for myself (my mom taught me this and I had to relearn it in my 30's).
- I work hard to have options.
- I enjoy philanthropy.
- I enjoy celebrating all my graduations, both grand and tiny…each mile and each invitation to the next room.
- As my husband says and I love: you can't force the piece of the puzzle into the picture if it is not right.
- Nothing is guaranteed, but thoughtful organization and flexible planning have been my keys to success.
- I love myself and enjoy continuing to find new ways to grow.
- Change is constant…I am cool with that.
- PATIENCE and knowing when to pull the trigger and take the risk…I'll get there and when I do it is always the right time for me, but I am quick to make a decision/ take risks when it makes sense.
- I trust my gut even if the study does not match…enough to be flexible
- I have a new 5-year plan in the works and successfully completed my last with a 1-year extension (ages 35 – 41). I was flexible, and I did it! Next chapter…to be continued.

- Money comes and goes…it is important to be able to take care of yourself and be accountable for the risks you take…
- My most valuable asset is my life and I am taking the time to appreciate and protect it.
- My priority is my family and they are my greatest joy.
- Positive energy breeds positive energy. Love more…
- I am so excited for the next chapter…bring it!
- My morning mantra: Rise and shine butterfly…it is time to meet the world!

Acknowledgements: A special thank you to my husband for his incredible partnership, to my parents for the priceless foundation that gifted me (you're the best), to my late brother – I looked up to you and still do, grandparents here and there for all of their time and love, to A.J. & the late Ivy for the endless love, to my best friends – my circle, to my incredible mentors Ed and Tom and to the Three Little Birds. You all brought me light when I did not have the answers and helped me find peace when there was none. To my nephews, Onofrio and Nino, I love you so much and pray for both of you daily to find your own path to happiness and peace. To my brother's friends, Bob, Pat, Becky, Richard, Anthony, Ronnie, Gus, Chris, Maria, Tony and others…thank you for keeping my brother's light alive with stories of his great character – I hear his voice and see him through all of you. To my extended family and friends – you know who you are - you have influenced my life so deeply.

I am blessed.

I am a Selfish B.

12 CHELSEA L. | IT IS OK TO CHANGE YOUR MIND!

My whole life I have been a people pleaser. Always putting what others want before myself without even realizing it. Growing up as the third child, I have always lived in the shadows of my two sisters and would have to constantly compete for attention. I saw my sisters constantly fighting with each other and all the negative attention they received for it and so I guess it came natural to me to avoid that behavior. I had been a goody two shoes growing up.

Never missing a day of school and I can recall one time that I tried to play hooky by faking sick in order to get out of school. I was soon scared to death when my mom tried to give me medicine for my fake ailment and immediately confessed because I was afraid of what would happen if I took medicine when I wasn't really sick.

Growing up as a perfectionist wasn't easy. No matter what compliments I received, my mind would immediately disregard and point out all the flaws instead.

When I was 14 years old, I saw my grandfather struggle through sickness. He was always in and out of the hospital and nursing homes until he was eventually overcome and passed on. Through this time, I always admired how nice the nurses were to him and my family whenever we were visiting. I observed how they could make us all smile despite the circumstances. I'll never forget the extra time the nurses took to explain things to us.

Although I was the baby in the family, my mom used to watch my two younger cousins every day after school and every weekday during the summer while their mom (my aunt) worked. I always felt like their older sister due to me being closer in age to them than I was with my own sisters. Which leads me to my young adult life and the inspiration to become a caregiver and to dedicate my life to helping others. I set my determination to make this dream of mine happen and started by taking every science class I could take in high school, applying to colleges with great nursing programs, and eventually graduated with honors with a Bachelor of Science in Nursing.

Although getting through school was not easy by far, having an emotional breakdown pretty much every semester, I stuck to it, despite the warning signs and what I think I began to realize subconsciously. I followed the advice from everyone else instead of listening to what my body was also trying to tell me.

I thought because I did everything I was supposed to do, go to school, get good grades, be polite, I had finally made it. My belief was that my whole life was about to begin and all the struggle I went through to get to this point would be worth it.

At first, I loved being a nurse. I loved being there for the patients, just as the nurses were there for my grandfather, and being able to be the one who could be the shoulder to cry on or the hand to hold when times were tough. It was inspiring seeing how strong people could be, even when faced up against the worst and still have hope. I invested all of me into nursing until I let it become me and would give a little of me to every patient until I had none of me left and became a patient myself.

After working as a Registered Nurse for about 6 months, I started having these symptoms where my heart would begin racing and felt as though it was going to beat out of my chest. With each beat it felt like a painful punch to my chest that in turn made it hard for me to catch my breath.

Going through nursing school and learning about the human body and diseases you can't help but to compare yourself to the symptoms you learn about and self-diagnose yourself with pretty much anything. I'm sure you too have heard the horror stories of people looking their own symptoms up on websites only for it to tell them the worst-case scenario which is in most cases completely incorrect. Well I attributed my symptoms to me working on the telemetry unit where cardiac problems were a large percentage of the patients I treated. Well as the weeks and months went on, I continued to have these symptoms and finally brought them up to my doctor.

I had testing done on my heart which all came back fine, and I began to criticize myself for wasting medical resources and over reacting when I had patients that I treated every day that needed so much help. The more I helped my patients the less I took care of myself. I started having panic attacks at work because I was afraid that I was going to miss some symptom or that I would make a mistake that in turn would harm one of my patients or even lead to their death. My anxiety made me a great nurse, I was always on top of what my patients test results showed, how they were feeling, their vital signs, how their families were coping with everything.

Meanwhile I didn't even give myself enough time to simply go to the bathroom or have a bite to eat in my 12-hour shift. My panic rose so high that I could not function before my shift. I would sleep all day and wake up with barely enough time to get dressed and drive in because if I woke up too early my anxious thought would snowball out of control. Just the thought of stepping into work would set me on a downward spiral of anxiety and I could not stop shaking, I couldn't eat, I couldn't sleep, I could not think about anything else except all the ways I could fail at my job, which would inevitably harm a patient, a human being. I would go into work shaking uncontrollably, red faced, tears in my eyes, nauseous, and tired until finally one day my manager would see me in this state and realize that I simply could not work.

I know she was doing what was best for all parties involved but, in my anxiety-ridden brain this meant I FAILED. All the hard work that I have put in for years, the many sleepless nights I spent studying. My whole life up to this point was pointless and I failed.

I could not, would not, wrap my mind around the idea of doing anything but nursing. Simply because it was what I decided when I was 14 and I would have wasted so much of my life trying to reach that goal. Meanwhile, I was using more time, wasting more life, doing what I thought I was supposed to do instead of doing what my body was trying to tell me. I had to come to the harsh realization that my lifelong dream was unfortunately not meant to be my reality.

What took me so long to learn was that expression that I'm sure you have all heard. 'You can't take care of someone else until you take care of yourself first'. You know the whole thing on an airplane where you should put the oxygen mask on yourself first before helping those around you? I realized that I had been going into work every day walking through the doors after having a panic attack for hours before my shift with 'no oxygen mask on' wondering why I couldn't breathe.

Walking away from my career in nursing has been the hardest decision I've made in my life, but it gave me time to take care of myself. In doing so, I've learned that its ok to change your mind.

Let me say that again, IT IS OK TO CHANGE YOUR MIND. Just because you made your bed doesn't mean you have to lie in it. Mess up the sheets! Walk away and find a new bed to make. Hell, find a cool chair to sit in for a while and relax.

This journey has taught me that your life is not set in stone. Routine is good but not if it routinely makes you miserable! Don't comply to the expectations of others because you want to make their life easier. Do what makes YOU feel good at the end of the day.

To share advice from a friend that I reflect on regularly:

"You are the one person who thinks about you the most so be the person you want to live with."

My advice to you: Don't go through life doing something because it is what you always wanted for yourself. Don't go through life doing something because it is what you feel you are *supposed* to do or what you've always *wanted* to do.

Do it because it is what YOU want for yourself NOW. If your dream changes and shifts along the way, know that it is ok.

I am a Boss.

13 DEANNA HENNESSEY | YES, ACTUALLY I CAN!

Hello, my name is Deanna. I am 53 years old and I live in Southern California. Here is my story.

I grew up on Freeport, Long Island, New York. I was the oldest daughter. My sister Michele was 7 years younger than me. Growing up, my family was pretty normal, I guess. I was 'The Quiet One' and always tried to please everyone. I tended to do what I was told.

I met my future husband, Greg, when I was 8 years old. We lived on the same street, about three houses away from each other. So, I guess you could say I truly did marry the 'boy next door'. Greg and I started dating when we were both 16 and we were inseparable from then on. We dated throughout high school. In November of 1984 we were engaged. In 1986 my parents moved to Arizona for the benefit of my father's health. Greg's parents moved to Southern California. This would be the first time I stood up to my parents. They wanted me to move with them, I wanted to stay in New York to be with Greg. They felt that Greg was forcing me to stay behind to be with him. This caused a lot of friction between my parents and I, but I decided to stay behind anyway. After a year Greg graduated college and unfortunately the pressure from my parents didn't decrease. I decided to move in with them in Arizona while Greg moved in with his parents in California. That's where he found his first job. We were married May 21st, 1988, in Arizona. We started our married life in Southern California. Greg was my soulmate.

Greg was not happy with his first job, being a firefighter is all he ever wanted to do. I was very afraid of him becoming a firefighter. He was a volunteer firefighter in Freeport, and I would sometimes be with him when a call came in and I would stand on the corner and watch them fight fires, it was very frightening to see. But after seeing how much he wanted to be a firefighter we talked, and he decided to become a paid call firefighter in California. I was still worried about his safety, but he talked to me and advised me to come down to the fire station during their weekly meetings and see how they trained so I did. I enjoyed it so much I became a volunteer firefighter with him for 5 years!

I learned how they fought fires, and this became something Greg and I could share together. After I started having children, I had to quit. During this time Greg became a career firefighter and he was finally happy in his job. Greg and I loved to travel all over the United States and camp with our boys. I wanted to travel outside the United States, but Greg was not comfortable leaving the US. This is where my love of travel started. I would say I'm more adventurous then everyone in my family. But because I was a mom and a wife, I chose not to do some more dangerous activities that I really wanted to experience.

As a wife of a firefighter you try to prepare yourself for that call that may come one day. But no matter how much you think you may be ready to hear something happened, when it does, your life falls apart. I got that call on January 20th, 2014.

At that moment all the plans we had made, our future together, everything had changed forever. The man that has been part of my life for 32 years was gone.

From that day on I had a choice, I could let what happened destroy me or I could do my best to stand up on my own. I decided my boys, even though they were 19 and 22, still needed their mother. I was not going to give in and give up the fight. I won't lie, the first year I felt like I was in a bubble. I didn't know which way to go or what to do. But both families, my family and the firefighting family helped me get through.

After the loss of Greg, I struggled to figure out what I wanted to do with my life and the lives of my children. I had to learn how to do everything on my own, how to pay the bills, how to take care of our home and so much more. The hardest thing for me was sleeping at night all alone and that is still a challenge.

I had to do my best to get through each day. I wanted to be strong for my children.

During this incredibly trying time, I felt something growing inside me. My rebellious and adventurous side was starting to emerge. So, for my 50th birthday I decided to go skydiving. Something I had spoken with Greg about, but he did not want me to do it because we had children. This was the first step in living my life the way I wanted. I also always had a passion for photography, even as a young girl I always had a camera in my hand. During a meeting with my photography club, one of the speakers was a wildlife photographer who shared that they had plans to Photo Safaris to Africa. Something inside me said I needed to do this. I was scared, I never did anything like this on my own. I decided to go for it.

This would prove to be the best decision of my life. A new world had opened up to me. The wonderful world of traveling has touched me in a way I never expected before. It helps me reconnect with myself, replenishes my soul and gives me the strength to continue on. I have been to several countries and I plan on traveling as much as I can and take as many photos as I can to capture these memories. I wish I could share these experiences with Greg but in my heart, I know he is with me. Also, when I travel, I don't shy away from doing adventurous activities. I have hot air ballooned in Kenya, climbed to the top of the Sydney Harbour Bridge, scuba dived the Great Barrier Reef, white water rafted in New Zealand. I look forward too many more adventures for as long as I can enjoy them.

The best advice I could give to someone who has lost their partner is to take one day at a time. Try to focus what's important for that day. It is also important to focus on yourself and to keep your strength up and your mind clear. That was very difficult for me to do in the beginning. I was so worried about making sure everything was taken care of. You need to realize that you can't do that if your body shuts down on you. You need to be strong to take care of others. You also need to find your passion, what drives you, what gives you JOY because no matter what you've been through, you still deserve happiness in your life. It's okay to enjoy the little things in life such as a nice hot bubble bath or a walk along the beach. Don't give up on you. There is a saying I love, it is, "Yes, actually I can". You can accomplish anything you set your mind to.

Never give up, never give in. You got this!

Life after Greg hasn't been easy and still to this day, I struggle with being lonely, scared, and not sure what direction I want to go. There have been other challenges as well. My oldest son has a health issue he is dealing with. I get angry sometimes because I feel I shouldn't be doing this alone. Of course, I know this wasn't part of the plan, so I'm doing the best I can. I am doing what my heart is telling me I should do. I get knocked down, but I make sure I get back up again. I follow my arrow even though some people may not understand me, this is what brings me joy. Me. I deserve joy. We all must understand that it's okay to make ourselves happy whenever we can.

I am a Badass!

14 AMY ROSE | MY BIGGEST FIGHT OF ALL

My life started as the daughter of a single mother whom struggled with addiction of any kind. Not knowing my life struggles would all be a product of this. I found I grew up too fast in some ways and in others, not so much. My mother died when I was 18 years old, leaving me to my grandparents. My family loved me and did the best they could.

Who I was came from learning from my mom. I learned that drugs and alcohol were wrong and only brought pain. But my need for love and feeling loved that she battled with, was going to be my biggest fight of all.

Entering my 20s I did whatever I could to feel happiness in my life. I moved to Florida to escape, being promiscuous with the opposite sex, and finding liquor. I did anything I was comfortable with to escape from feeling unloved, never understanding that I needed to love myself in order to truly know what happiness felt like.

I was in and out of relationships all my life. I was also changing jobs constantly. It seemed I'd never settle down with either. If something came along and it was seemed too good to be true, I would find a way to ruin it. Subconsciously I didn't think I deserved to be happy. I don't know when it happened but the feeling of wanting more grew inside of me so much, I just had to pay attention.

I no longer wanted to just work to get a pay check and I no longer wanted to date to feel loved. I found love for myself little by little and slowly it fueled me to want more. I moved out on my own and had to enjoy my own company, something I feared for the longest time. In the silence of my mind, I grew into a woman at age 30. I became more independent in every aspect of my life, confident in what I wanted to do with it. I began to finally realize that I was built for something far greater than what I was living up to.

I no longer wanted the loss of my mother to allow for the excuse to not be better than my best. I'm not perfect. I'm still not where I want to be, and I still struggle with all relationships.

I spent years learning about myself so that I could find a career I love. I found my self-worth and learned to be good to my body. I'm happy with my life and it feels amazing!

It's never too late to become a Selfish B!!

I am a Selfish B.

15 KRISTA CIMINO | PROVE THEM WRONG

My journey up until this point in my life has been a winding road with lots of uphill climbs and downhill falls. I grew up in a crazy home environment.... lots of drug and alcohol issues with my parents unfortunately. I lived ashamed of what went on behind closed doors, not letting too many people into my home for that reason, pretending my life was like everyone else's. At the age of seventeen, I got pregnant. Looking back at it now, I understand why everyone was freaking out about it, but at the time I knew I was going to be a great mom.

The more people that told me I couldn't do it, the more I could not wait to prove them wrong. My son is the reason I am who I am today! He is my angel. He has kept me focused and driven. Every decision I made was driven by what was best for him, which in turn created the best life for me as well. I've overcome so many hardships including lots of health issues that started as a young child. I've suffered the loss of a parent. I've gone through a divorce which was the hardest decision I've ever had to make.

I've also had the most amazing moments as well. I was able to start a career that I have an extreme passion for, and I have worked hard every single day, put in lots of long hours, took classes etc....to become great at what I do.

I opened my own salon business in 2012 and have continued to grow so much in the last 6 yrs. I have the most amazing team of hardworking ladies! I am truly blessed in life and I embrace all of the things I've had to go through because I am a firm believer that there is a reason for everything you experience...good or bad! Everything I have endured has made me an unbelievably strong woman who knows if I set my mind to something and am willing to work hard than I can achieve those dreams!

We need to learn that we are just as important as everyone else in our lives and we need to take care of ourselves just as much! It's so important for our body and our minds!! We can do anything as long as we are healthy and happy!! It all starts with us.....

Since, opening my salon, I have been blessed to meet so many different women from all walks of life and make them feel good about themselves. I strive to bring out their own individual beauty. I have formed relationships with them as if they were my own family. I listen to their insecurities, hardships, sadness and happiness all in the few hours they are in my chair each month. I'm so blessed to be able to be there in any small way that I can.

I think as women we need to be building each other up, not tearing one another down. We need to support one another - always! We have one life to live and we need to make each day count. We must find happiness even if in small amounts every day!

Gina, you are so right!! It IS ok for us to be a little more selfish.

I AM a boss and I've learned it's ok to be a "Selfish B". Thank you for opening my eyes. I am a happier woman because of it!

GINA CLAPPROOD

16 C.B. | I AM A RECOVERING PEOPLE PLEASER

As I reflect in my thirties, I think, wow have I changed over the years! When I was in my early twenties, one of my coworkers said to me, "Just wait until you're in your thirties! You won't care as much about what others think about you. You'll understand who you really are as a person and will learn to cut a lot of bullshit out of your life. And wait till you're in your forties, it's even better!"

At the time I really didn't understand what the heck she was talking about and it scared me to think about being thirty or forty-something. Now being a thirty-something year-old woman, I now understand, and she was SO right! It's AWESOME!! I am understanding my authentic self and I love who I've become. I've had a lot of bumps in the road that have shaped me into who I am today, and they have forced me to grow and change. At the age I am at right now, I feel strong, physically, mentally and spiritually more than I ever have! I've worked so hard to get to the healthy place that I am today. I'm certainly not saying that I'm perfect by any means. I will always (and I mean always) be a work in progress because we are always learning and growing. I work hard on myself now, by choice.

However, in the past, it wasn't always because I wanted to but because I HAD to. I had to because I hit such a dark horrible place that I had no choice but to crawl my way out to slowly learn how to help myself and begin building a healthier, happier me. Life has taught me many valuable lessons along my journey. Suffering through anxiety not knowing what the heck it is and thinking you're just "weird" and "different" throughout your elementary and teenage years causes lots of uncomfortable feelings. You can't talk about it because heck, how do talk about something you can't figure out or understand what it is?! I hated school. I mean HATED. Never thought I was smart enough, struggled in school and easily gave up. I had friends and enjoyed parts of socializing but man, social anxiety kicked in every time!

Fast forward to college. Yes, the kid who hated school since 7th grade went to college; to be a teacher! Ha! I became a teacher, so I could help other kids, like myself, who hate school and think they're not 'good enough'. In college I started to learn that I better figure out strategies to help me get through college or I wasn't going to make it. I learned I couldn't hide every time I had to present in front of a class. I couldn't skip out on classes when I felt like I was having a heart attack because my heart was racing from anxiety, and the list goes on. This was when I started to realize, I have to help myself.

In my early college years, I dated an older guy who I had a crush on for years. Thought we were in love and this was 'it'! Took me years to figure out the guy was an alcoholic. It's true what they say, 'love makes you blind' to a lot of things. The twenty-something year old, naive, unhealthy girl back then, missed every sign. I think because I didn't want to see it and I also didn't understand addiction. I also always saw the good in everyone. Long story short, a night of a severe beating left on the side of the road, a restraining order, tons of individual and group counseling, weekly Alanon meetings, I left for good and never looked back. This was the second time in my life where I had to work on me.

This was one of the hardest and saddest lessons I had to learn. And boy, there were many lessons that I learned through this period in my life. Even when the relationship was over, counseling, meetings and working on myself was not over. In fact, it was just the beginning of really finding my authentic self. I graduated college, got a job right away as a teacher and was really good at it! It felt good to have worked so hard and to feel I was (am) really good at my job! I met my husband who was a breath of fresh air! I was on my toes looking for any indication he was an addict of any kind. Never, did I ever want to make that mistake again!

We bought a home together and completely gutted the place to make it what we wanted to be! It was both mine and my husband's first time moving out of our parents' homes and first time being on our own! Sadly, only a couple of months after moving in, we had several days of disastrous flooding and our newly renovated home with new everything, was filled with over 6 feet of water. We lost just about everything, including my husband's new truck. Although we were devastated, thankfully my husband still went on with his original plan to propose to me a week after the flood!

With help from our family, we cleaned, gutted the place for the second time and rebuilt our place into a home once again. Then we planned our dream wedding!

This life lesson taught me not to give up! Getting married to my now husband was one of the best days of my life! Everything was amazing, and I was so happy to be married to someone I deeply loved and knew he felt the same about me. Sounds like a happy ending but you know life likes to spice things up and challenge us! But now looking back and knowing what I know now, life does that to us to teach us things and to have us grow. So, I grew… I always wanted to be a mother. Tried for a child right away after getting married! Finding out I was pregnant was incredible and I was over the moon happy! I ended up miscarrying and did so naturally at home and it just so happened on the same day as the Boston bombings. Such a horrible and depressing day all around. We waited a while to be emotionally ready before trying again. I got pregnant very quickly, but sadly miscarried again. This time not going through the loss naturally because I couldn't emotionally go through it again that way.

This experience taught me many lessons such as patience. We can plan all we want but life does not always go as planned. I had no choice but to accept that my plans did not go the way I wanted them to at the time and I had to be patient. I eventually had my beautiful, healthy rainbow baby and it was one of the happiest days of my life! My life completely changed for the better and made me want to be an even better, healthier person so that my son could grow up watching what a healthy person looks like.

I worked on my life more than ever. I wanted to give my son the best life I could possibly give him and that meant having a healthy, happy mom who knew how to take care of herself; her whole self. My life got even better when I welcomed my second son a couple years after. I call him my miracle baby because right up until he was born, we were told and prepared for my son to be delivered with a missing piece of his intestines. Had plans for surgeries, long hospital stays and so on, but he came out as a healthy, happy, beautiful baby boy! To this day, doctors don't know what happened. During that pregnancy I was sad at times over the news of my son having health issues yet was so hopeful and patient with it all. I think because I had learned years earlier that I will be able to deal with whatever the universe throws at me. Also, patience and positivity really do wonders. Becoming a mom has made me feel so whole inside. It has made me want to just do better with each day.

I still to this day see a counselor. It helps me focus and concentrate on me. When mommy is healthy, calm and happy, so are my sons. My mental, emotional and physical health affects my family. I now CHOOSE to see the positive side of people, situations and with life in general. I have learned the hard way, what kind of people I want to surround myself and my children with. I have learned to cherish people who love me and to let others go who don't. I've learned there's a big connection between physical, mental and emotional health. I try to exercise my body as well as my mind. I choose to do what's best for myself and my family and to not care about what others say or think I SHOULD do. I know best because it is MY life. I get to choose who and what is in my life. Choosing who and what is in my life involves the word, "no". For my own sanity and mental health, I have learned when to say no and I just recently learned not feel bad about it! I have to say no to events and people even when they may try to make me feel guilty or less than for doing so. Before, I would cringe with guilt and anxiety because I would feel as if I was letting someone down or felt I needed to do this or that. I now know I cannot please everyone and the only people who matter most is myself, my sons and my husband. I've learned to do things because I want to, not because I feel guilted to.

I am a recovering people pleaser.

Lastly, I have learned to tune out negative commotion and focus on the positive. I've learned to listen more with less talking. I've learned to value moments and memories rather than things. I've learned to never stop learning and growing. There is always a lesson(s) to be learned from every situation, good or bad. I've learned to do things that make ME happy. I've learned with counseling, exercise, eating a healthy diet and constant self-reflection, that I have never felt better. I truly believe without these hard life lessons that I had to go through, I would not have learned these valuable tools to guide me through to a successful life.

Through these good times and bad, I have learned my true self.

I wholeheartedly feel and KNOW …

I have become **a SELFISH B.**

17 N.D RISLEY | BOLD BIRD

In order to paint the landscape of one's life, one must be willing to get messy in part, and unwilling to leave out the textures, layers and colors that shape it. My landscape, oh, what an unremarkable piece it would likely be had it not been for my willingness to burn it to the ground, fertilize the soil and lay down new seed. It was the later work which laid the foundation for it to become the landscape it grew into. To paint one's landscape of a lifetime, one must tend to that landscape with a bold vision, great passion and the discipline a landscape requires. Yet few stand well-remembered once we are transposed from this plane to another. This is a material world with material goals, needs and desires. All those physical things have an expiration date and that is fine as long as we remember what we are trying to become. And as ever we are here to discover ourselves, and in doing so it is inevitable that we eventually return to the dust from which we were born. The truth of the matter is that before that eventually the average individual is lucky to know of a handful whose lives they truly touched. Some of us may experience the privilege of affecting more of an impact, if only for the sake of a bigger purpose. The most powerful aspect of these opportunities is the absolute clarity with which we have the ability to each understand our role. Once understood it is with total acceptance that one must take on such a responsibility. Our lives and voices are created to be big and if lived well they will be heard and they will echo with resounding layers as time passes by, reminding us of our place within the universe as conscious and willing practitioners.

In the moment you recognize and accept your purpose, a certain calm settles on your shoulders. It is something not exactly but akin to relief. You are ready for life to happen. You realize you are simply a part of many parts, but a part in a whole to which you belong. The self no longer matters. Life becomes in those moments, a malleable, transient substance to which you are able to be on par, and as you suddenly become equal to this substance, not in size or depth, but in a collaboration of balance and intention, and an understanding of the way things are, you can form a partnership with the Universe and all that is if you are willing. It is a partnership you choose in order to employ the ability to create with it.

Eventually, the unthinkable lands in your life, just as it happened to your cousin, or your neighbor, or your best friend. You are unable yet to wrap your mind around the idea of what is happening. You would consider the act of altering something but which something is crucial. How does one alter one's experience in life when all we are doing is moving along the conveyor belt of life? When we venture to make a choice or to take a leap, choose a path, deviate from the path, drop the ball, rise above, venture forth or crawl inward, that is when we get an answer, that is when we begin to know who we are. But it lays dormant like our sleep until we ask. Until we are ready to know.

The day my father died a black crow found its way into the house me and my once husband owned. I heard it come in as I slept and then when I woke up at dawn to go see what all the racket was, it flew past me fast and landed on the kitchen window sill. I screamed for my husband to be to come get it.

Then I said, and he will corroborate, "Oh, my God, something happened. It's my dad."

Seconds later, the phone rang. It was simple as that.

It's all about perspective. Or as they call it in showbiz, it's all about POV, that is, point of view.

I learned about POV very early in life. My father, a scientist, an entomologist to be exact, had a particular way of seeing things that either fascinated or frustrated me, depending on how I was affected. His POV intrigued me always. My father, whom everyone called The Professor or Prof would always say, "Just decide! You decide you want a thing, you go after that thing. It's a decision."

When I would say, "It's not that easy".

He would reply, "No, it's not. But it is as simple as that."

I didn't understand then, but I do now. We each create our own reality, and in order to create the reality we desire we must choose that which we want. We have to understand that it is up to us and we must commit to the decision. He lived applying this concept and I know for a fact that this was how he created his life experience and I thank him for not making me expect it would be easy, because it hasn't been. On the other hand, he didn't explain the specifics of how a total mindset shift would be necessary. Perhaps he didn't break it down that way, because it was just as natural to him as breathing. Or maybe he struggled with that part too. I knew mind power wouldn't be easy, because easy was never my father's way. But difficult never deterred him. For that matter, neither did impossible.

I learned to appreciate his point of view as I grew up, and as I watched him achieve great things. He made incredible leaps in his area of science and won lots of awards and accolades, none of which he ever spoke. My father never achieved for the glory, he pursued his dream. He had dreams but to him they were not dreams, they were visions. He was a visionary and to him things that had yet to been proven, authenticated or published were not impossible, they were awaiting discovery.

My father died in Nairobi hospital after suffering horribly during the weeks leading to being admitted in the intensive care unit. My mother said that after months of frustrating dry coughing and feeling tired or run down, a hoard of alarming and confusing symptoms finally took him down. My father who wasn't sick a day of my entire life was admitted to intensive care. After countless exams resulted in reports which continued to baffle the doctors, they finally submitted an X-ray, displayed a chest cavity overrun with cancerous ulcers. They were quite blunt when they declared that at this stage there was nothing to be done. The cancer was far too advanced. Three days after he was informed, my father succumbed to his new reality. He went to sleep and never again woke up.

His death was a massive blow to me. I had foreseen that it would be, had always feared I would have to find a way to withstand the pain of this loss and there it was. My hero died and I was the spoiled little girl who had refused to acknowledge the gut feeling that she should go home when she had the chance the week before, the day Auntie Grace called her to give the news that Daddy was ill. Why didn't she heed her inner voice? Because he couldn't be sick. Because she had asked if he wanted her to come home and of course he said no, and she had chosen to believe him because it was easier than facing the fact that he might need her and that it might be the last time she would see him. Why? Because in many ways, she was still a little girl. I was still a little girl and I was still in that stage where bad things didn't happen in my life. I was too young to believe it could be otherwise. In truth I was thirty-three years old, going on thirteen. I didn't know it then. I felt pretty grown up and why not? I moved from Kenya to California at seventeen, all by myself, but I had been supported by my Dad my entire college run and I have to admit, for several years after. I was given an easy ride so when he said he was fine, that I should focus on what I was doing, and he would be on his feet in a matter of days, I chose to swallow his answer. I took his answer, though his voice was faint, and he didn't sound at all like himself, and I used it to fortify my denial. I "just decided" he was going to be fine because he told me so. Of course he was! He was the "the Professor." He was my Dad. He was fine. He was fine because he had to be, and because I was afraid to go home.

Five days later, that I was afraid was irrelevant, I was on a plane home. I went alone just the way I wanted it. I didn't know what to expect and I wanted to face whatever confusion or battle it was going to be alone, without a witness or someone else to take care of.

My fear was not unfounded for nobody bothered to warn me that it was going to be an open casket funeral. I stared at the waxen face on my father's reclining body and felt fear and awe simultaneously.

It took me a long time to recover from that. Years. And it was the trigger I had been dreading. During the funeral service I was a complete mess.

My mother passed the baton on to me just before I was getting ready to board the plane back to the States, back to my home. Back to my once husband. Back to my two beautiful, mini pins, my four-bedroom San Fernando valley house with the black bottom, kidney shaped pool in the backyard and the two-car garage in the front. I was returning to my life in the valley, the life my father had wanted for me. My happy needy dogs awaited me. They needed me. My clients at work, they too needed me. I needed to home to me. I wanted to get away from all of what had been laid in front of me and that included my mother.

My mother, the most lovely human being possible. She was my father's beautiful bride and a selfless, generous, loving, effusive mother to her five offspring. I loved my mother. I did. But she drove me stark raving mad most of the time.

We had the typical difficult mother-daughter relationship. We were too alike with exact, opposite points of view. My mother's why was not only to serve but to nurture. Why because it made her feel good and because she had a huge heart. And because she needed to feel loved especially in a world where her husband's needs were always considered before hers, always overshadowing her as smarter, more important, more interesting, always more.

I grew up in many ways doing what she did. But I wasn't doing it from a place of needing to get love. At least that's what I thought at the time. I thought I was doing it to help people help themselves.

I got paid to help, I didn't get conned into giving and getting nothing time and time again, as she did. I didn't want anyone relying on me. She loved it when they needed her. Of course, nowadays I see that there are more similarities between us than differences. And the judgements I made, well they were hardly fair though they were true but they in many ways applied to me though it was impossible for me to see it at the time. That you should know the story of my mother and me is important in your understanding that I took the things my mother said very seriously but it doesn't mean I liked hearing them. Perhaps it was because my mother was rarely stern and when she was, you could not afford to ignore her. True story: she was also almost always infuriatingly right.

That day before I left, my mother said, "You are the one. Out of all the kids it's you. You have the greatest chance of following in his footsteps. But you need to stop playing around. You need to figure it out."

That was it. She dropped a bomb right on top of me minutes before I was to say my goodbyes.

I was elated and I was livid. How could she throw that on me? What kind of parting gift was that! And I told her so. She gave me a look shrouded both with love and annoyance.

She said. "Stop whining and do what you know you were meant to do, mummi", using the endearment like a whip. "Stop! Stop fighting it. Your father knew it too. You are the one he was looking to."

I left feeling the power and weight of what she told me. I left deeply saddened by my goodbye to him and even more so my somewhat lukewarm good-bye to her. I felt saddened that we left each other with no words of support between us. Yes, I told her I would do what I could. Yes, I said I loved her, and I would make them proud, not knowing anything anymore. Not knowing it was the last time I would see her alive and a little more than two years later, my beautiful, generous, passionate, loving mother's life came to a quiet end.

It took me ten years before I self-imploded. I began to understand what my mother had tasked me with. Through that learned that you cannot deny who you are and knowing that can save you or bury you alive. I lived a long time buried and then I awoke. Shaken by a series of losses, denials and rejections, I was forced to go back to the drawing board and start my life all over, start it right from scratch.

I have yet to do exactly what I believe I must, but I am in the process of building that thing. I have a purpose and a belief and belief is a powerful thing to have. I have much to do but I'm okay with that, I'm happy with it for I get to be me all the way. I get to be me on purpose, on point and on my way to having everything I choose to experience. I'm not doing any of this for anyone else's dream, not for the expectations of others, not for my own ego. I'm doing it for many things, to answer my curiosity and my desire to live. I want to know what's different in me, and what's the same. What's possible for me and how far can I go? How many people can I affect and how can I help them grow? What's my POV now that my life's directed? Is it broad, open and receptive or is it narrow and focused and braced? All I know is you can't go high while aiming low, and that failure isn't failure unless you quit. And you can't take in the new if you can't let go of the old, and you must forgive yourself if you ever want to heal. But most of all I truly believe that anything is possible. In fact, I don't just believe it, I'm counting on it.

I won't lie, it's been anything but easy. I sometimes wake up in the morning, drenched in a cold sweat, and I'm back on the floor of the motel room I shared with three others some years back when I imploded and moved away. Sometimes I remember walking on that hard ground in that hard town knowing a hard life was all that remained in front of me and despair enveloping me like the sea drowning me in a tidal wave.

But then I look around me and the sun is shining, and I see a fly buzzing around the window, and it settles on a curtain and I don't move to swat it away. Instead I stare at it and I smile, and my heart begins to warm up as I let go of the nightmare. I say to the fly, "Dad was your friend too. He saw your importance. He saw your possibilities." The fly is rubbing his feet together, calling out to other flies. I know all this because Prof, my Dad, shared these things with me. He talked to me about his fears too and he trusted me for my guidance. To him my guidance was magic, and it was real. And now that I can see that I live in awe and in gratitude. I can believe it to be true, that he knew something in me that no one else knew. He knew long before I did what I could be, what I could contribute, my something to give the world. There is something to be said for learning to love yourself. It is no easy task. It means digging into who you are under the rocks and bringing the trash to the surface, all the secrets, and mush. But the prize is treasure you never knew was a part of you. And left is fertile ground in which you can plant a few very special seeds. There is a wealth of growth to be had if you water those seeds and give them the love time and attention they need. I am no little girl, I am a woman with a gift and a purpose. I can afford to be bold. In fact, I can't afford not to be.

I saw a jet-black crow recently. It was pecking at the window of my bedroom. It was calm and observant, and it stopped when I sat down. It didn't move. We locked eyes. I thought, Pretty bold! And then I smiled to myself. Bold Bird!

Yes, I am indeed. I am a **"Bold B."**

18 MUGGLE | OWN IT

Gina requested I write about my success in life. After giving her request an enormous amount of thought, I decided I would simply write about what makes me who I am. In one of my communications with Gina she stated simply "own it." At that time, I was unsure of the consequences of her request however I now understand I must own it. I am me.

I was raised in the south – Florida to be exact. I grew up in a traditional family with mom at home and dad working. I was taught by my parents to respond with "yes mam, yes sir, thank you and please." I complied. I attended Roman Catholic school grades 1 through 12, learned not to question authority and to listen more than speak. My father ruled with authority and violence – spanking was allowed. While I feel my mother did not agree with the violence, she complied given she was raised in a similar environment. Unfortunately, the patriarchal society dominated my world.

Prior to graduating from high school, I decided to speak with an Air Force recruiter about enlisting – I was curious about the military as an alternative to college. After graduating from high school, I began taking classes at a Community College while working full time at Walt Disney World. I thoroughly enjoyed my employment at the Magic Kingdom but the stress from working and attending college took a toll on me. I felt I did not have support from my parents because they were immersed their divorce which was filled with anger and unhappiness.

Off I went into the *Wild Blue Yonder*! This decision to enlist in the Air Force forever altered my destiny. Oddly enough, when I was young, I felt strongly I belonged in the northeast, which is why I wrote 'New York' on my dream sheet for destinations while in Basic Military Training School. My knowledge and understanding of procedures in the military was greatly lacking and because of my upbringing I did not inquire about the ramifications of writing New York on my dream sheet. As I reflect back, I can clearly see how the events kept unfolding to benefit me however, while forging through I was not so happy about my situation. The Air Force motto at that time was "it is an adventure" and for me it truly was.

After Basic Training in San Antonio, Texas I was flown to Denver, Colorado where I spent over a year attending school specific to the aircraft and system I would be working on. Even though my training was intense, I was determined to succeed. While attending school In Colorado (Lowry AFB) I met and married my first husband. Once my education was complete, the Air Force moved my new family and me to Plattsburgh, New York. My hopes of a bright future in service were immediately squashed upon my arrival at my new duty station - I met my Shop Chief, MSGT. Jones. Sergeant Jones was a good-ole' southern boy who made it very clear to me I had no place in his shop or in the military. I was made to listen to his constant insults, sexist remarks, and blatant off-color jokes while working. I was the only female in the shop during day shift. I later learned women who had been assigned to this shop had asked for a transfer or become pregnant and discharged from the military. I did neither and felt trapped but knew I had to endure – I signed the papers to serve my country, and I was not a quitter. Day in and day out it was very difficult to be bullied by MSGT. Jones. I kept reminding myself it was not forever but some days I felt defeated.

I did however have one very good experience while stationed in New York. MSGT. Jones lost his mother and father within a short time period causing him to be absent for a couple of months. While he was away dealing with his family tragedy, the base was undergoing an Inspector General (IG) visit. This period of time in our country's history is known as the cold war and even though there were no active wars, we played war games constantly. This included working 12-hour shifts day-in and day-out with little time off – many times I worked weekends too. War is war. During the inspection of the shop where I worked, the IG noticed a neat and organized supply log and inquired who was responsible. The acting Shop Chief shoved me to the front of the line and said my name loudly. I nearly fell into the Colonel's lap – it was embarrassing and a nice icebreaker. The end result was being mentioned by name in the IG report, which was framed and hung on the wall over MSGT. Jones's desk – by the acting Shop Chief! I attempted to transfer out of my duty station to another job many times without success. My husband at the time knew how I was being treated daily and saw how I changed into a sad and defeated airman. Unfortunately, he made a decision, which altered much of my future - he forged documents in a package meant to be a new beginning for me and instead caused me to receive horrible punitive damages. My career in the Air Force was ruined and my marriage was never the same. I was interrogated and treated like a criminal receiving a horrific punishment. My place of work was never the same to me after this experience. In the end, I was able to transfer into the Air National Guard and I moved with my family to Boise, Idaho to another new experience in the military. After being in Idaho for a short period of time I was contacted by a company in southern California to work as a contractor. My future boss interviewed me after I picked him up at the Boise airport and offered me the job! I moved to New Hampshire and worked at two bases in the northeast with quite a bit of travel monthly. I eventually ended my marriage because the trust was gone between my spouse and I – he turned to drugs and became someone I did not like. This new job gave me the opportunity to move forward once again.

My life took a new twist. In my new position I traveled to different bases and reported information to the Air Force about

equipment and money spent to modify and perfect these machines.
I enjoyed my new job as a government contractor – I felt liberated
and was confident in my role. While working at one of the based, I
met a man who would become my next husband and the father of
my children. He was active duty Air Force and directly involved
with the equipment I gathered information on. We had been work
colleagues – then friends. Our friendship developed into very
good relationship and we eventually began dating. Four years after
we began dating, we got engaged then married and began the next
phase of our lives together as husband and wife.

We had decided on a traditional marriage – both in agreement I
would stay home and raise our children – he would support our
family. At the time I had no idea how much I would relinquish my
sense of self and independence. I simply did as I was conditioned
to do; listen and obey. While these words sound harsh now, at the
time I did not realize any of this.

I was happy for the most part – I had always wanted to be a
Mommy. Staying home with our children was wonderful and

challenging. My children remain my biggest and most important accomplishments - I have learned about and from them in ways I never imagined. That written, my sense of self began to diminish the more years I spent not completing what I longed to do. I felt lost in a world I could not escape. My husband had his work and his travel. He was able to associate with adults and move about interacting with others on a daily basis. I barely had time to learn about the daily news. If and when we did communicate, it was always with the knowledge work was first. I understood I came second at best. I did not realize how my self-confidence lapsed until the death of my father in 2009. It was at that time I finally saw what I had become, and I was not happy who looked back at me in the mirror. I tried to correct the wrongs by working on my marriage, but it was too late. My mind was made up and I was done trying. I felt I gave all I had to give and could not go back to the person I was who always gave in. I needed to be first and to come first. I felt an old familiar strength rising inside of me.

My parents told me from a young age I was very strong-willed and confident. I wanted to be that person. I decided I would use the same inner strength I found to deal with MSGT. Jones; I ended my marriage, sold our family home, completed my Bachelor's degree (Summa cum laude), found a full-time job and began to rebuild my life as a single mother of 3. It was not easy, but I persevered. Failing was not an option and I am an optimist.

Eight years have since passed. Two of my children have graduated from college and have terrific professional careers; an architect in New York City, and a Licensed Social Worker in Boston. My youngest is an Aerospace Engineering major in his sophomore year in college. I have purchased my own home and have a wonderful job. When I sit back and reflect on the course of events that led me to my current path, I cannot ignore how my inner core kept me from veering off-course. My strong coping skills and "quitters never win, winners never quit" attitude over-ruled any defeatist ideas. I can sit back and see my good choices and praise myself for staying focused. It would have been far too easy to give up. Today I am happy and have a peaceful inner feeling.

What do I feel successful about? First and most importantly I must mention my children – they are my greatest success and I am extremely grateful to be their mother. I continue to marvel at the strong adults they are and enjoy spending as much time as I possibly can with each of them. I am also very proud of my service to our country. I have two honorable discharges and am currently in counseling via the Veterans Administration to assist with the trauma from my experiences while stationed in Plattsburgh, NY. My goal is to increase my disability rating for monthly disability compensation – they owe me. The trauma I experienced daily has caused anxiety symptoms to manifest in my current life. My education is a huge success story in itself; I completed my degree from the University of Phoenix while raising my children and dealing with my father's mental health decline caused by dementia, and his death. While enrolled in school – I was chosen to make an Internet advertisement for the University of Phoenix, was flown to Los Angeles to film the commercial – all expensed paid. I successfully purchased my own home using my V.A. benefits – it is all mine! I successfully ran and was elected to serve my community twice as a School Committee member (total of 6 years). I thoroughly enjoyed this experience working in the community for our greatest assets, our children.

What advice would I give to other women? Be still and listen to the inner voice – never ignore it. Once you hear it, go with it because it will never steer you wrong. Turbulence reminds us what we are truly thankful for – embrace the turbulence! If something is not what you imagined it would be, change it. We have a responsibility to ourselves to be the best; be it a mommy or a scientist. I feel we have one body to house our beautiful soul and it is our responsibility to nurture and take care of our bodies - take the time to take care of ME – words I never heard as a child. We have permission to explore all options and to be happy. My happiness is my choice.

I am a Selfish B.

19 LAUREN S. | THE DEFINING MOMENT

The Beginning... I think when we are given the task of choosing a defining moment in our lives, we immediately gravitate towards the "big ones". For me, that was definitely my original thought and trust me I have many to choose from, both happy and devastating. When it came time to sit down and choose though, I decided on what was a seemingly innocuous choice that ended up becoming one of my greatest life accomplishments.

Nine years ago, my oldest son was given an Autism Spectrum Disorder diagnosis. During his initial stages of therapy, it became clear to me and his therapist that I may need some support of my own, so I decided to start some private therapy sessions, separate from our family sessions supporting my son's diagnosis. At the time, I thought this was just some extra support to help me as a new mom navigate a difficult, confusing diagnosis, and that it did. What I didn't know is how these sessions, which continue to this day, would help me to build the core person I am today.

Although this journey of my defining moment begins with my choice to start therapy, there is a bit of a back story that is significant and worth sharing because I feel that I, like so many others, waited so long to seek treatment out of guilt and shame. To keep it brief, as a child/adolescent I suffered from multiple forms of abuse mainly sexual and emotional. It continued for years, the sexual abuse into my teen years and the emotional abuse well into adulthood. I never dealt with either of these issues until beginning therapy at the age of 30. I had no idea how greatly it was impacting my life until I began treatment, in fact, I never even admitted to myself or anyone else that I had been abused until I started filling out a questionnaire at the start of my therapy. The reason I chose to share this piece is because this was the first step and one of the hardest parts, at least for me. Moving past the stigma of "going to therapy" and embracing all it has to offer can be an uncomfortable first step but if you are brave enough to take those first steps the rewards are infinite.

The Road to Becoming a Fully Functioning Adult.... When I first started therapy sessions, I was functioning, emotionally, at the level of a five-year-old, scared little girl. I sat with my therapist week after week feeling completely lost. I was incompetent and unable to make decisions for myself without considerable self-doubt, questioning, and more self-doubt. I had no trust in myself, no idea what my values were or what I believed in and why. I didn't know how to feel or how to really allow myself to "feel". Many days I was so anxious and distraught I could spend large amounts of time pacing the floor to calm myself and help cope with whatever triggered that moment of anxiety and distress. I felt like I was a passerby in my own life. I just went through the motions. I was a good wife, mom, employee, and overall human being but I didn't have my "Why". I didn't have my core values figured out, so everything seemed a bit muddled.

This vicious cycle went on for years and it has taken years for me to be able to share my experiences with you from this perspective. Even just a year ago I couldn't have imagined I would have made it to where I am today. Fast forwarding through 8 years of healing, forgiving, growing, developing, and discovering I have my WHY and my defining moment! My core values are so deeply a part of me, they are reflected in every choice and decision I make. No more self-doubt, no more checking with others for reassurance, I know what's right for me because my values lead my choices. For the first time in my life I am proud of who I am, I know who I am, without a single doubt in my mind. I know what I stand for, I know what I believe in.

I have found peace in forgiving those who have hurt me. For me, that forgiveness comes at a distance, but it is pure, which is the most important piece. I never thought I would want to be just "me". I spent so many years looking to others and emulating their qualities. Waking up these last few months and truly loving who I am has been the most amazing gift.

Healed AND Healing... Every so often I have an experience that reminds me that healing is a journey, not necessarily a destination. I do feel that you can be mostly healed and have pieces of you or parts of your story that are still in the healing phase. This happened to me recently at a doctor's appointment. I was having some testing done, it was two phases but going into the appointment I was only aware of the first phase. I was nervous going into the appointment when I was aware only of the FIRST phase. It was a semi-invasive test, lasting about an hour, but the information that could be collected from the testing was incredibly valuable so it was worth the short time of discomfort for the results it would provide. Once I checked in and realized there would be a second phase of testing, that was then explained to me in detail, my anxiety went from manageable to off the charts in a matter of moments. Had this same scenario happened a couple of years earlier, I would have been unable to complete any of the testing, my anxiety would have escalated to the point where I would have left before the test began. I would think of any excuse to reschedule the testing for "another time". At this point in my healing though, I was able to complete the test. This was a huge win for me. I felt amazing and sick to my stomach all at once... proud of myself for my "win" in the first phase of testing and overcome with anxiety for phase two which was immediately following. The thing about abuse triggers is that they creep up on you when you least expect it. My abuse had nothing to do with any of my doctors. It didn't occur in a clinical setting, but I have a very specific trigger, that happens every time I have a particular exam done by any doctor other than my own. The first test, although invasive, was set up in a way that did not trigger a reaction for me. The second test involved lying on a table setup for a GYN type of exam. Even when I am prepared for this type of exam with a doctor other than my own personal doctor, I have the same trigger and what I call a "left-over" reaction of my abuse. It has taken many years of working with my doctor and gaining her trust for this reaction to disappear during HER exams. Needless to say, when I went into this appointment totally unprepared for this procedure, my anxiety was high. I tried all my usual coping mechanisms. Positive self-talk, "this is a safe place, these are doctors, this is what they do, lots of good information will be found from this test, etc." They began the test; the doctor was not the best at communicating to begin with and before I even realized it had started my reaction had begun. Anytime my legs are "unwillingly" put in that position, the position that requires being in stirrups on a GYN table, they automatically start shaking uncontrollably. It's not a conscious thing, it's a physiological response that I have absolutely no control over and I cannot stop it from happening once it starts.

This doctor was very insensitive to this response and repeatedly asked the nurse to stop my legs from shaking. That's about all I remember from the exam. He did some talking about what he saw during the procedure but when I'm triggered this way I automatically go into my own little world. I glaze over and retreat into my head, unable to process anything that is happening around me. It's the only way I get through it. It's my world, my safe place. It's the place I lived for so many years and it was my normal.

Nothing outside registered with me, I thought this was just how life was supposed to be. As the exam ended and I tried to pull myself back to reality, I needed to use the restroom before leaving, my legs were still shaking and I was still numb and retreated in my own space, processing very little of what was going on around me. Typically, in the past, I could stay in this world, this space for extended periods of time. It was safe for me, I enjoyed being in this space and "feeling" this way or not feeling. This time things were different, I'm a different person, a stronger person. My "world" helped me get through my triggered moment, but I no longer wanted to stay there. It didn't feel right or good to be there anymore. I got in my car and sat there for a few moments until I felt like I was back. The fact that I was able to come "back" before even leaving the parking lot proved to me just how far I've come in my healing process. I was triggered, I had a response, but I no longer was the girl I used to be. I didn't want to stay in that numb world anymore. I wanted to get back to being the true me, the core me. In that moment I realized it's ok to be healed and still have moments of healing along the way. It's not weakness but incredible strength that allows you to be both.

The Silver Lining...I want to end with some words of wisdom that my therapist recently shared with me. She said "Lauren, if you have nothing to ever hold you down, you would just float away." This was in response to a recent time of increased stress I have been experiencing. I feel like people who have been abused or through trauma tend to see things in black and white. We have trouble dealing with stress after finding happiness in fear that we may never be able to find that happiness again. At least this has been my experience.

A huge piece of my defining moment has been the realization that we are all a work in progress, and that's ok. It's ok to make mistakes, it's ok to have a bad day, week, even a bad few months. It's ok to forgive yourself the way you would forgive others. It's ok to be HUMAN.

I am a Selfish B.

20 VICKY HAMAK | NO – THAT DOESN'T WORK FOR ME

As a business owner, for years people would take advantage of me because I was always the "yes" girl. Always trying to make everyone happy and not rock the boat. Employees and clients would take advantage of me because I would let them. I was everyone's doormat. Turning the cheek and agreeing to everything and letting things slide to keep the peace but in the meantime, it was affecting my business, my self-esteem, confidence and happiness. I lost myself and I didn't know who I was.

I was dating a guy at the time all of this was going on and caught him coming out of a restaurant with another woman holding her hand and they were kissing. I was destroyed. I didn't know what to do or where to turn. I was so depressed I just laid in bed and cried.

As I was paging through my Instagram one day to try and numb the pain for a while, I came across Gina Clapprood's page and instantly emailed her desperate for help because I didn't know where to turn or what to do. Gina emailed me and from there, with Gina's help, I slowly started picking up the pieces. I started loving myself (which previously I had no clue how to do), growing a backbone, and learning to say, "No" in a nice professional way.

I have lost some friends in the process of my growth and learning to love myself and put myself first, but what I really learned is they really weren't true friends to begin with. And the guy I was seeing has made several attempts to get back together with me, but I have kindly said, "No, that doesn't work for me!" He's with girl number three now.

It has been exactly a year now since I had first emailed Gina in desperation and I can proudly and confidently say I am kicking ass; my business has grown and is very profitable and productive. I am a very professional confident women that will not be anyone's doormat. I am so proud of myself for the growth I have obtained by standing up for myself, loving myself, my confidence, my self-esteem, and my kind professionalism. Saying, "No, that does not work for me," has never felt so good and empowering and I owe all of this to Gina Clapprood!

Thank you, Gina! You truly are amazing, and your books are amazing! Thank you for everything!

I am a Selfish B!

21 KARA ST. ONGE | A FRESH START

I have lived most of my life trying to please others. Making THEM happy would make ME happy, right!? My greatest struggles have been in relationships. I had one long relationship where everything was my fault…traffic, the weather, you name it, it was my fault. After three years of dealing with trying to please him and make him stop emotionally abusing me, it hit me one day – I NEEDED TO CHANGE FOR MYSELF!

I changed the genre of music I listened to, got a self-help book and bought my first home 40 minutes away to have a "fresh start". IT WORKED!!! I felt like myself again! I was so proud to be twenty-two and have a mortgage and a good job!

Then I met the father of my son. Two months into the relationship, I found myself becoming bossed around, yelled at and sometimes pushed around. I ended that really quick! I went through my entire pregnancy ALONE and it felt amazing! Another change in my life that I did on my OWN and felt proud of!

I then met my husband. I love and adore him. He adopted my son and helped in raising him since he was 6 months old. He was loving and attentive and so amazing. It was a fresh breath of air since my last two horrible relationships!!! However, his ex-wife was fixated on making our lives a living hell. After a couple of years, ups and downs, I decided to take the higher road and befriend her. Why not right? This would hopefully make our lives much easier, and the kids would be happier because of it.

But then I stepped back and realized, I have this wonderful blended family that I love so much, but OMG! I'm doing it AGAIN!!!! I am putting all of THEIR needs first and I'm the one not sleeping at night, running around crazy and super stressed out!! So really, is it worth it?? NO.

I made the toughest decision of my life. I decided to be a Selfish B and moved out of my home. I took my son and dog and lived in a tiny apartment that I HATED. But I wanted to make myself happy. I didn't want to come in between my husband and the stepson that was jealous of me. I walked away. I tried hating him.

I tried being the "better person" for THEM. Give THEM the relationship they wanted without me getting thrown in the middle of it… I decided that I am no longer going to help my husband be a better father and help my stepsons with whatever they needed…they had parents, right? Now, please don't think I am the stereotypical evil stepmom. I feel as though I am not painting the best picture of myself here, but while I loved my blended family, I just couldn't take the stress of being a target anymore.

As the year went on, I really, REALLY missed my husband!! He's my best friend. I realized I couldn't breathe without him in my life. So, I brought out the Selfish B in me again and said screw this!!!! I refuse to let an ex-wife and one stepson ruin my life, ruin my FAMILY.

My new outlook on life now is to be the Selfish B that I know I can be! I took a huge step back! I no longer talk to the ex-wife to make sure she's happy and not threatening us. I blocked her number from our phones! I no longer step on eggshells around my stepson, I just refuse to be in the same room as him!

My whole life, I wanted to please everyone…well guess what! I'm here to please MYSELF and to make sure I'M happy and healthy first! A weight has been lifted off of my shoulders and my marriage is better for it! My boys are happy! It might've taken me half of my life to get it right, but I did, and it feels amazing!!!!

I love being a Selfish B!

22 STACY A. WARNOCK, BA, RN | LOVING

YOURSELF BACK TO HEALTH

How can we discover God's role for us if we do not allow
ourselves the opportunity to learn to love who we are
imperfections and all? If we share our struggles with mental
health and suicidality then we are not alone, different, bad, insane
or wrong because we know others have not only experienced what
we have but they have also lived to share it with others.

My Dear Child,

First, I wish your view of life and of yourself, was not so

dramatically bleak, because I see something so different. As if the

lenses we are looking through are remarkably different divulging

diverse reflections. I see through my lens a strong, beautiful young

woman with countless tremendous opportunities. Life is filled

with loss, fears, battles, illnesses, deaths, and disappointments;

however, these events are completely out of your control. I sense

because you fought so hard to survive for so very long that you tire

so much quicker in battling the necessary aspects of adulthood. I

believe it is in your best interest to make peace with your inner

soul and spirit. You currently are an adult woman, BUT you are

accepting and attaching to old messages such as being damaged, dirty and disgusting. It is so vitally important that you not only disbelieve these old messages but that you let them go, like a child letting go of a balloon and watching it rise in the sky until it is gone. Instead of being imprisoned by these old memories and beliefs, just notice them mindfully as they occur, ride the wave of emotion until the water is calm. Learn to be real and get in touch with your genuine desires.

Life is NOT a continuum of just accomplishments or failures, please do not base your choices on the chance of having to face your imperfections. You continue to compare your inner self, values, relationships, spirit and soul to other peoples' new cars, homes, pictures of their children and vacations. Comparing insides to outsides is like apples to oranges. These past few years you faced what was real for you, no approval or validation is needed from others. I am so very sorry it was such a painful, isolative and disorienting experience, but it has served great purpose. When you climb a mountain the physical demands of the uphill battle make the view from the top sweeter, and the downward journey more appreciated and serene. You have been faced with many battles to fight. It is tiring, but you are a courageous warrior. In the past you have lived to care for, rescue and please those surrounding you. No, you should NOT live your life FOR others. However, hiding in your bedroom not asking or sharing what is real with those who love you further isolates you making taking one's life a very real possibility. Connection with your friends and family helps you prove how special you are. Isolation reinforces the mental illness, the being different, the idea that there is something wrong with you. Part of the largest difficulty with feeling so alone with suicidal thoughts is we fear, that not only are we very different but so different no one else would comprehend. Choosing to put your feet on the floor and lift your head ready to face the day reinforces your purpose for the day and contributions to those around you. Whether it's your laugh, or your love of animals, or an empathetic ear for a friend or creating art or poetry there are methods you contribute to for those around you. Careers are not the only place to discover purpose but because you are on a break from nursing it gives you the gift of time to grow and explore. When you are unable to love yourself with kindness and compassion remember your Higher Power who loves you unconditionally and continue working on growing love for yourself instead of hatred, or harsh judgements.

A very large share of individuals remains extremely judgmental regarding the act of suicide. Many believe suicide is selfish, or even utilized as a weapon to hurt loved ones. The truth which is often hard to accept is counter intuitive. There is a deep, dark, frightening, and desperate pain. A pain one only knows or completely understands if you have been there in that hell. One's heart, brain, spirit and soul believe suicide is the only way this overwhelming pain will end. The American Association of Suicide Prevention lists suicide as the tenth leading cause of death in the United States illustrating the severity of mental illness and poor treatment modalities or problemed access to help someone feeling unsafe.

I am a survivor. I am a warrior. The one incident which had the capacity of ending everything was my extremely serious and very lethal suicide attempt. There are only a handful of people whom have known my truth. However, I am no longer terrified to share the hell I have been through and slowly traveled back from because that is an accomplishment of amazing proportions, and if my truth benefits just one person by encouraging them to ask a trusted person or professional for help than sharing honestly is my choice.

Quite ironically, I am a Psychiatric Registered Nurse whom assisted individuals battling mental illnesses or suicidality. I am a very talented nurse, quite versed in caring for others from a very young age. However, self-care was not valued or modeled for me as a child, so now as an adult I am lacking the basic skills of true self care. I was viewing this as a way out of my dark depression. How many years of complete denial does it take before your body starts telling your truth without any approval from your heart, mind, spirit or soul? This system worked for me, until it reached the point of no return. I did not allow myself to go past a certain point emotionally and attempted to fix what is broke on the inside with outside rewards. Maybe if I bought a new car? Maybe if I lost weight? Maybe if I bought that new house? Maybe if I applied for a new job? Maybe if I stood on my head? One of these things could be the start of my journey to happiness, right?

GINA CLAPPROOD

So how did it all go down? I started my new job in November of 2012 as another attempt at a fresh start not only in my career but also in my life. From the time I began my job I was bombarded by circumstances out of my control which affected not only my ability to perform up to par at my job but also emotionally I started falling apart, bit by bit. Within a two-month period, one of my precious pups died while the other ran away for 48 hours in a blizzard. There was a tragedy, a school shooting, at a local elementary school which robbed me of what little hope that remained. I became ruminative, obsessed with the true tragedy these families were facing. I had a type of survivors' guilt on a new level because I wanted to die, and I was left alive. Yet God decided these children who wanted to live should not only face death but face death in a painful and horrible method. I was distraught over my circumstances, including financial concerns, my inability to have a baby, a very rare and somewhat untreatable cardiac condition, a new autoimmune diagnosis, a multitude of inpatient psychiatric hospitalizations secondary to trauma, depression, anxiety, and my overwhelming sadness and my desire to take my own life. Ideas of giving up on life enveloped me. Planning on how to take my own life often circulated in my mind and I ruminated on how intolerable my life had become. Nevertheless, I was making it to therapy one to two times a month. And the therapist of whom I had seen for seven years, sent me an email stating she could no longer work with me. My cardinal fear not only abandonment but by someone I trusted who knew most of my secrets, but also a woman who had promised to walk this journey with me as I would not trudge this road alone.

I had struggled to live life. I worked at accepting that I had to alter plans secondary to the chronic cardiac condition which has greatly affected my physical abilities and limitations. Postural Orthostatic Tachycardia syndrome (POTS) is a form of Dysautonomia which refers to a group of diagnoses involving a dysregulation of one's autonomic nervous system. Anything controlled automatically by my nervous system is affected. It took me eight years and nine cardiologists prior to receiving a proper diagnosis. Unfortunately, a diagnosis did not bring a solution I hoped or prayed for. If the doctors could label it, they must be proficient enough to treat it, right? The problem is this was a new diagnosis and very little was known regarding how to treat POTS. I had ongoing issues with major changes in my blood pressure, heart rate, breathing, digestive issues, dizziness, fatigue, fainting and increased anxiety and depression related to isolation and inability to function at same physical level. I continued experiencing an inability to manage my cardiac symptoms without successfully not allowing my illness to affect my entire life, and certainly not my new job. Then the next things to affected was normal everyday activities of daily living such as walking, heat intolerance, position changes, physical and emotional stress, dehydration, showering, climbing stairs, any exercise, as all had the ability to lead to my fainting.

An emotional pain so evil it took my breath away. I was in such a pain it is hard, no almost impossible to explain to someone who has not experienced it. Depression is NOT just sadness. It is a pain that is all-encompassing, overpowering, profound, dark and deep, bottomless and never ending.

I did NOT attempt suicide to passive aggressively hurt anyone else. It was totally and completely about me and only me. I wanted to end my pain, and I had arrived at the last stop reminding me the only way to end the pain was to not live anymore. On January 21, 2013 I had been walking to my car on the campus at work, as a car sped by suddenly my thought was to jump in front of it. I pushed the thought away as I had been doing previously with these thoughts for months, maybe years. When I arrived home, I was already sobbing, and I could not help myself nor could I ask for what I desired because I truly believed no one could accurately give me what I needed. I needed to take away that pain, for once and for all. I sat down and quickly swallowed 250 extra strength Tylenol. I lay on my bed with my dogs and suddenly I began questioning this action, my choice. I told my fiancé whom rushed me to the nearest emergency room. As the nurse was taking my vitals, I began apologizing to her for my overdose and she looked baffled as to why I owed her any explanation. Soon it all went black. I was to be life flighted to an urban hospital an hour away however it was not possible secondary to a snow storm so instead they transported me by ambulance with two state police escorts. The next I remember I awoke with my fiancé and his mother, my parents and my brothers at my side. I could not talk because I was still intubated, had a nasogastric tube inserted and I had no idea where I was or why. To be perfectly honest when I discovered what had happened I had very mixed feelings and thoughts regarding surviving an action of which I prayed would end this knot of pain growing in me and indescribable. I spent a week in the intensive care unit, a week on a medical floor both with a person watching my every move to ensure my safety. And then a week on the psychiatric unit, a challenge was for me to experience a psychiatric unit not as the nurse but as the patient. This required me to access a great sense of humility and know this was all a part of my journey. I had to stand in line for medications unlike as the nurse having full admittance to the medication room. I felt as though I was standing on the wrong side of the nurses' station. I did not lead the groups though I was expected to participate as a patient. I was not able to eat my lunch brought from home but forced to sample the hospital food. I was not able to leave the hospital, or to leave the floor, I was a PATIENT on a locked unit on the other side from where I usually stood.

Even with my experience as a psychiatric nurse inpatient, outreach, clinic and visiting nurse I still frequently ran into roadblocks and found it near impossible to navigate this system. A system where patients, people needing gentle and all-encompassing care, fell through the cracks.

What lessons availed me? I believe I am a kind, compassionate, intelligent, spunky, sarcastic, unique, beautiful warrior. I have fought to all ends to not allow my depression to steal my life. I had numerous hospitalizations, therapy, trauma therapy-progressive counting, transcranial magnetic stimulation (TMS), psychiatric medications trials, Dialectical Behavioral Therapy (DBT) and I still saw no light, had no hope. I was left with the only other option being electroconvulsive shock therapy (ECT). For two years every other week at 5:30 am I was driven to the outpatient surgical unit to be put under anesthesia, so I could have ECT which is documented to have a greater success than medications in treating depression. Basically, while you are under anesthesia the psychiatrist hooks you up to have an electroshock which causes a seizure which is thought to have better results than medications or any other treatment. I have not been psychiatrically hospitalized for 15 months nor I have I had ECT for 10 months though I remain on an extensive list of psychiatric medications and participate in twice weekly therapy.

Life is difficult for everyone. I will pass along the piece of advice that those people we think are normal are fighting their own battles, some are clearly evident, and others are hidden beneath layers of secrets and cosmetics.

I am a Selfish 'B'.

23 HLA | A PLACE OF PEACE WITHIN MYSELF

Somedays I honestly don't know how I've gotten this far in life. I can say that it's NOTHING like I dreamed it would be...NO fairytale here. I have experienced many obstacles, let downs, heartaches and I'm still standing. I'm finally in a place of peace within myself. I'm not looking to please everyone anymore by "walking on eggshells", I did that for far too long.

I get it, no one wants to be the Bitch, but do you really want to be the rug? I think not. I know because for most of my life I was the rug. I was always the one who NEVER said no, and I ran around ragged trying to please everyone else. Here's an example, I have a girl friend who I'll call "N", we are great friends when she doesn't have a man in her life. When she is "alone" she calls, wants to make plans, etc. The minute she finds a new flame she's nowhere to be found. Don't get me wrong I'm happy for her, but she seems to leave everyone else behind until the breakup. When the breakup strikes, here she comes wanting to make all sorts of plans, shopping, walking, dinner, lunch whatever it may be to keep her occupied. The thing is I'm tired of being the "backup", don't call me JUST when another man has left. For a long time, I would try to reach out and make a "dinner date" every so often to catch up, but now I'm done.

Friendship is a two-way street, if she doesn't make the effort, neither do I anymore. I mean come on I have a lot that goes on in my life and when she needs me, I have always been there. I have rearranged my schedule to accommodate yet another person who needed me.

Well I'm sorry (not sorry) to say that this girl is fed up with people who don't make any effort to maintain the relationship. Does that make me SELFish? Maybe I just don't feel the need to put in effort in these types of situations any longer. Don't get me wrong, I don't always say no now, but I try to take care of me first. It's taken me a long time to get to this point. My life isn't the fairytale I dreamed of, it's far from it, but it's my life.

I am a Selfish B.

24 JACKIE R. | LEAP OF FAITH

I first met Gina at an "Intuitive Session" at a friend's house. I liked her immediately and was impressed with her intuitive abilities. Several months later, I received an email from her regarding the other services she provided including being a Life Coach. At the time I was very unhappy in my job in the Hospitality Industry. I felt like the environment was toxic and was affecting my spirit. I wanted to quit but my husband encouraged me to stick with it, and said I was only three years away from full retirement and the time would go quickly. For a while, I agreed to stay in the job and tried to keep a positive attitude. I looked at job postings daily and decided to update my resume. I contacted Gina to help me with the process. During this time, I also signed up for monthly Life Coaching sessions with Gina to figure out what I wanted to do and how I could make changes to live the life I wanted.

I took a leap of faith and quit my job the week before Christmas. I was immediately relieved and did not feel fearful, at any time, that I would not be able to find a job even at the age of 63!

I took off the month of January to "re-group" and started to look for a part-time job in February. Because I had worked only full time during my life, this was a big change and I did feel a little guilty, but felt it was the right thing to do for myself at this time in my life. I now work part-time from home, doing office work for a local company, which is exactly what I wanted to do. My hours are flexible which allows me to play golf weekly in an early morning women's league. I also have time to meditate and exercise before starting work, meet friends for lunch, and go to my grandchildren's school functions. I am no longer stressed out and feel like I am living my "best life"! I do not think any of this would have been possible without the support and coaching from Gina.

I guess you could say she helped turn me into a **Selfish B**!

**Note: Since the writing of my story, I realized that, although there were many benefits from working from home, I missed the social aspect from working outside of the home. I decided to take another leap of faith and leave the position after ten months. I am currently enjoying each day and looking for the next best opportunity!

25 HEIDI MARKARIAN | THE UNIVERSE HAD OTHER PLANS

My awakening began in early 2000. I call it my awakening because I didn't truly know the strength that I possessed and still continue to draw from. I left my native Texas to move to Rhode Island on a whim to live with my then boyfriend. We hadn't been dating very long but had been in the same circle of friends for years. I was really taking a giant leap of faith but knew that if I didn't take this chance I would wonder "what if" for the rest of my life.

Moving and living in a new city was a trying time but one that I embraced. Truth be told it was one of many trying times that would come my way. I loved exploring a new city where I didn't know a soul and could do things with a certain amount of anonymity but that soon lost its luster. I found that I missed the familiarity of my home, family and friends.

Although I settled into life and eventually got married my path would take another turn. I had my first child in 2006 and it became clear that my husband and I were on different paths in life. I desperately wanted a family and the last thing he wanted was responsibility. He wasn't around much, and I often felt like a single parent. As much as I tried to put on a brave face and carry on, I couldn't keep telling myself that things would get better.

Our divorce was finalized in 2008 and it was honestly one of the lowest points in my life. There is no guidebook for divorce and the avalanche of sadness that overtakes you. At that time, I didn't know anyone that was divorced, and it felt like I was alone on an island. In the end it felt like your memories of your married life is undone in minutes by a judge's gavel. My family was 1700 miles away and thankfully I had a good support system of friends in Rhode Island, but I still felt like I was swimming upstream every waking moment.

Things gradually became easier however, I still felt that pull of my family and my roots. I began to seriously consider relocating back to Texas and had gone back to visit my family in the spring of 2010 to work on my return. When I returned to Rhode Island from my trip, I remember telling my best friend that I was headed back to Texas. I hadn't met anyone of substance and thought that a change of scenery might help me and my son. Little did I know that the universe had another plan in store for me.

It was in the summer of 2010 that I met my now husband. We were set up by friends and had planned on getting together over the fourth of July weekend. That weekend came and went with no call from him. I remember thinking "how dare he stand me up" and for some reason, felt compelled to call him on it. We agreed to meet, and my plan was to make him realize what a great catch I was and then never call him back again.

Once more the universe had other plans for me. I remember being instantly drawn to the sparkle in his eye and how easily the conversation flowed between the two of us. He has such an amazing heart and was/continues to be my rock. Fast forward 8 years, we now are a family of five and life has certainly thrown us some curve balls, but I am confident that I will continue to muddle my way through. I might not always pick the easiest path but in the end, I know that I can and will find a way to make it through. My advice to my younger self would be, don't give up on yourself you will pull through. You've got this! **I am a Selfish 'B'.**

26 JEANNE OUELLETTE | A WORK IN PROGRESS

I was raised by an overbearing, unloving and physically abusive narcissistic mother. I spent my life trying to please her and make her happy. It took me years and a few thousand dollars for therapy to figure out that nothing would make her happy because she was unhappy with herself and projected that onto everyone and everything around her.

My reprieve in life finally came when I was a freshman in high school. I met my best friend, my newly found sister. We were inseparable and soon became more like family than friends. Zully's family, especially her mom, my mom now, accepted me, loved me and treated me like family. I was now one of seven, loved children instead of a lonely, only child. It was in their home that I learned what it's like to be loved unconditionally, what the love of a mother is supposed to be like.

Although I had this wonderful family to support and love me through any obstacle, the damage my biological mother caused was still looming and I was too damaged to really recognize it.

I looked for love and acceptance anywhere I could get it. I was overly kind and giving to anyone I met. If my love wasn't returned, I tried even harder because I thought I was doing something wrong so of course I had to fix it. Needless to say, this yearn for acceptance followed me into adulthood and every relationship I was in. I had my heart broken more times than I care to remember. It was when I was twenty-one years old that I thought I found my salvation. I met my now ex-husband. I thought he was everything I wanted. He was only everything I ever wanted as long as I worked extra hard to make him happy. I figured out years later through therapy that I married my mother, looking for the acceptance that I would never get, nor did I truly need from anyone but myself.

My marriage lasted twenty-three years. I like to think that not all of those years were negative. Throughout my marriage, I tried so hard to make my husband and his family happy that I continued to be blinded that I wasn't happy. He verbally and emotionally mistreated me because he was unhappy and depressed because of his awful childhood. He inadvertently looked for his family's approval by mistreating me because they didn't really like me and made it known. I was never good enough.

I begged him for love and acceptance for years. He would yes me to death, but never followed through. Of course, he always found a way to blame me, everything was somehow my fault.

My marriage was on a downward spiral because I was just getting so sick of being mistreated. I just couldn't take it anymore.

I finally had the nerve to walk away when my ex-husband got physical with me and then our daughter one night during a night of his drinking and an argument. I won't say it was easy, nor will I say my kids didn't suffer through it, but we are all much better now and getting better every day. My motivation for leaving my husband is my daughter. It's important to me that she knows it's not okay to live in any kind of relationship where you are mistreated.

I'm still a work in progress, but a strong, independent work in progress. I'm learning to accept myself for who I am, love who I am and persevere. This too shall pass, and I will overcome.

I am a Selfish 'B'.

27 NICOLE TARTAGLIONE, LPN | THE

SELFISH NURSE

"As a nurse, you know that every day you will touch a life, or a life will touch yours." -Unknown

What is the definition of selfish, you ask? Or maybe you're not asking, but I am going to tell you anyway. It's an adjective and according to the internet it's defined as "lacking consideration for others; concerned chiefly with one's own personal profit or pleasure." Hmmmmmm....

Now I read this to myself and say ... "Me!?" That is so not me! Unless *maybe* when it comes to sex?! I mean, I am chiefly concerned with my own orgasm... and don't tell me you're not either. And please keep that between us. Ha!   Anyway, how can I be selfish? I mean I spent thousands of dollars to become a nurse to serve and assist others. Selfish would be the last thing I would ever be called, and trust me... I have been called many things. Some of the synonyms listed for the word 'selfish' include egotistic, self-centered, self-regarding and self-loving. Self-loving you say? Well that doesn't sound selfish right? For me, I can definitely say I love myself, why is that a bad thing? They say (who is they anyway? Million-dollar question, right?) you have to love yourself before you can love anyone else, so how can that be a selfish thing? I'm confused. I am sure you are now too. Sorry.

Being a nurse, (besides the sex thing), has made me realize how selfish I am. I do what I do for the feeling it produces inside. Like an addict does for the rush, the high. Although what I do to get the feeling is not illegal, I possess a license for it. I have the best job in the world. I do what I do to please others. To get the hugs, the tears, the thank you's. I crave those feelings. That is all I want.

If you ask anyone in the world, they would say a nurse is one of the most SELFLESS human beings in the world, and it's true. But we are SELFISH. We have to know we've helped you, changed you, made a difference, or it's all for nothing.

God bless my fellow nurses, and all whose lives have touched us. We are Selfish B's!

I am a Selfish 'B'.

28 MARIE K. | DON'T SETTLE

As I sit and think about my life and everything that has changed in the last few years, I am amazed at how strong I have been and how much stronger I am now! When they say you are stronger than you think…it is true!! The world and some relationships have tried to break me, but I have come out stronger!

Several events have changed me over the past few years, from a crappy job that almost broke me to the death of my mom.

I read a quote once that said, *"Say how you feel. Leave the job you hate. Find your passion with every ounce of your bones. Stand up for things that matter. Don't settle."*

A few years ago, I was comfortable at my job, it wasn't an "easy" job but the people I worked with were like family. Well, when a new job opportunity came along, I was happy where I was and didn't want to leave. I began feeling pressure from my personal life to take the job due to more money, and pressure from a coworker because the new job came with a lot of stress that she didn't need.

Instead of being, a 'selfish B' I let her keep the job I loved, and I took the new job. Everything went downhill professionally from there. There were many times I had to stand up for myself in this new position, they didn't know me, and they didn't know my heart. I tend to be naïve and trusting…well that job cured me of that. When I tell you that I thought at one point they had broken me, I mean it! I would come home in tears and sob because of the way they made me feel. In the end, I moved on to a new position and to my surprise was greeted by some wonderful new co-workers.

I know most of that sounds sad, but in the end, I made it through a terrible experience that I honestly thought at one point I would not. I made it out better and stronger. I learned to be more selfish and take care of me.

When I desperately wanted to leave my job, like most people, I worried about how that would affect my family financially. So, I stayed longer. I've found that in life, events happen that force you to make "that" decision. You know that the one you wanted to but weren't strong enough to make on your own. I ended up getting injured at work and could not do my job any longer. Blessings in disguise. I have learned a lot about self-care since leaving that job.

I am healthier and happier now. There is no going back. Every event in life, good or bad shapes us, you have the choice as to how it shapes you. I didn't let that job destroy me, Instead, it shaped me into a stronger person. I believe it helped me get through my mother's death.

I learned so much about self-care and thankfully, I was able to practice it while grieving. I'm not saying grieving was easy, I'm saying I took care of myself and allowed myself to grieve in my own way.

I let myself find joy in the little things even though my heart was broken. You see, I learned if I don't take care of me, no one else is going to.

I truly learned to be a Selfish B.

29 ANDREA FOUNTAINE | BE A 'PEACH'

Well here it goes. I feel different moments have defined me at various stages of my life. One of the my first defining moments was when I was in elementary school. A classmate started saying to me, "don't go pass go, don't collect $200.00". He was speaking about the fact that my father was in Federal prison. To me it was my norm, so I never knew that it was a negative thing that he was in prison.

Another defining moment was the moment I realized that I was a mom. Even though I carried my love for nine months and labored for thirty-three and a half hours, just to end up getting a c-section after all that, it was the first time Devin's little hands touched my arm. Instant bond of love.

I believe we were home for maybe a week, and we fell asleep. It was a deep sleep and his little hand rubbed my arm again. I jumped up because I thought it was a spider (my enemy) and there was my sweet baby boy smiling in his dream touching my arm.

That was the first moment I fell in love. The purest form of love one could ever feel. I was in awe of being a mom-his mom.

Another defining moment that I didn't understand when it was happening at the time, were the words from my sister's father-in-law a.k.a 'Papa'. He used to tell me in Italian, "you can be the ripest peach but there will still be someone who does not like peaches". Going through my baby daddy drama and feeling low about myself, I wondered why he would say this to me, and why say it now?! It took me some time to truly recognize the power of that statement and didn't fully make sense until I got older and wiser.

I will never forget when my son and I went to the beach (not my favorite place) and before we hit the sand there were two young female teens and they said, "oh poor kid, imagine having a mom look like that" (I was a little fluffy). I carried this with me for years. Until the moment where I had the realization that you can be the most fit, young, and absolute picture of perfection in your eyes, but there will always be that effing person that has something to say. So be a peach and let those who love you love you and eff the rest of them.

And now my most defining moment was the day prior to losing the strongest woman in my world. My mom. The day before my mom left us, she had fallen off her bed. I was so frustrated because all I wanted her to be was the strong woman, she taught me to be. Here she was is in this pathetic situation on the ground all night. A lot transpired in a short amount of time, but when it was time for us to go, I was so mad I did not want to kiss her. All I could hear was her saying to us, "never leave this house without giving me a kiss goodbye". So, I did. And that was the last time I ever got to kiss and hug her.

My life will forever be redefined. The little things that people worry about no longer matter to me. And as for any bullshit that comes my way, I will not tolerate it. Each day is a struggle but another one of my mom's sayings to us was, "put your gloves up Rocky and go another round".

If you were to ask me what I have learned about myself the answer really is, I just don't know!!! I have been so focused on taking care of my son and making sure he did not become another statistic. In staying focused on that, I lost me!

I know that I am a good mom, daughter, aunt, friend etc. and it pains me that I don't know me! I have now learned from writing this contribution that I have a lot more to learn and I deserve to explore more about who I am and love myself unconditionally as my mom loved me.

I am a Selfish 'B'.

30 GINA MILAZZO | IT'S OK TO FEEL BROKEN

"It's OK to feel broken, Gods Shaping You"- My Transformation to becoming a Selfish B.

As I sit here in the woods, camping, reflecting in writing, I feel a little uneasy. Two things come to mind that got me through many of these days. It's OK to feel broken because God is shaping you, and it's OK to have moments like this - but just try not to have days, weeks or months that linger on like them. When you feel this way, not only have your emotions got the best of you, but your soul starts to shine a little less bright. This is the time to stop. Stand up to your potential!

Show yourself that you have the capacity and the right to be calm and develop into something much truer to your future self. For many years after high school, I felt the need to please those around me, my family, my friends - even strangers. Who am I kidding? I still do this at times not realizing that you should always focus on pleasing yourself first.

Be that Selfish B that Gina writes about and heed the advice that it is not selfish - it is self-respect and knowing your self-worth.

This didn't come very easy for me to change in fact it almost cost my life. What I'm about to write next is very personal and this subject is not discussed in my life. Please bear with me through this journey.

I had the honor to sit down with Gina to talk about what opened my eyes to a clearer picture of what and who I am searching for. We talked about many topics I could write about for this book, from having my first son at only eighteen years old, married, divorced and getting through many unhealthy relationships, to the many health problems and surgeries, the loss of a handful of my very dear friends at such young ages. The light, the dark, and everything in between.

I know so much that what should share here may have the power to impact just even one beautiful broken soul. And show them that they are worthy of living.

Here is goes. Then came that one day. That one day that I was worn down and weary and although it wasn't just one day for me, it was days, weeks, and months that built up. That's when the downward spiral happened, right before me unknowingly. I craved that satisfaction of those awful curse words that wouldn't leave my mind: I felt everyone would be better off and likewise if I died.

The thought of eternal peace came with no emotions. I set out my intentions to end my life. There are many things I wanted to get in order as I dropped my third little guy off to preschool, I remember hugging him so tight. Oh God SO TIGHT and said goodbye. I wrote letters to each of my boys. And had everything ready and organized.

If this may sound like you right now, STOP. Cry. Feel. Yell. Know these moments are OK and find faith that some higher power, for me that's God, is shaping you.

God was shaping me, and I had lost total sight of that. Yet, even that didn't stop my intentions. I was completely numb to everything, no emotion but maybe a single teardrop.

If you know me, you know this is not my character. I'm as emotional as Robin Williams in Patch Adams. Working for many years as an emergency 911 operator, I had many tough calls like these and always thought, how could someone get that bad to be that selfish? Or what can I do to really help them get through this right now? Well I know now it's not about selfishness at all.

So, I'll go back about two months before the spiral - I was feeling blue, sad and unmotivated so I went to a doctor and guess what? They pushed the meds. Now I'm not saying some people should never take them, but for me I don't even like to take an ibuprofen. With that said, always follow your gut. In my case the doctor insisted and said, "no no take this you'll feel so much better". Yeah right. Not for me. If any side effects were to happen, it would be to me. The thing was, I had no idea it was affecting me in such a negative way. The side effects were silent.

I kept thinking, this must be that 'calm' the doctor talked to me about. It was great to not *feel,* or so I thought. So back to my last day, which I now call my 'aha! Moment' thanks to Gina. I told her this story and she was like "That's it! That is your defining moment."

Of course, I was so hesitant to do so as I never even discussed it with my parents, my kids, my family or my friends, but when she said, "Gina you're amazing and could help someone else going through this", I was game.

That day, that fateful day, my mom Betty came knocking on my door at 9 AM, which she never did. God's plan. She came in and asked if I was OK and I had numbingly responded yes ma'am. But you've heard of mother's intuition. Moms know. So, she insistently kept asking me and finally, I fell down to my knees. I began to sob. I sobbed like Victoria Falls in Zimbabwe.

Somehow, I pushed through and immediately went to see an amazing counselor who I see regularly now see for about the last five years. Tracey, if you're reading this, thank you. I can never thank you enough. Many times, I wanted to throw in the towel and end the struggle. The thought of not being worthy to be alive - no more. It stops now. So again, if you are reading this and ever felt or feel similar to this and you have more days, weeks, months, or years like this, and not just quick moments, a breakthrough is coming. You're amazing and one day I would love to hear your story of unleashing your 'B'.

I discovered so much about what made me feel alive and healthy. What makes me sad and feel alone in a crowd. I took charge of me. Now I call the shots. Even through the toughest time, the toughest days like today, my head is a lot clearer and I know I'll be OK.

I am driving this vehicle, with the help of God of course. He really is the ultimate Savior through this. Now, I just put on my headphones, open up Pandora and listen to some good ol' gospel radio. Find your Pandora. Find your God.

Thank you for allowing me to share a glimpse of my journey. You've got this. Don't give up because there are things to love about you and if you forget what they are, find an old friend and go out with them even if you haven't talked for years. Laugh and find a piece of you that was missing. For me, I sometimes just sit listening to music for hours on a day off without feeling the pressure of I should be cleaning, with the kids, or with the husband.

Be selfish at least once a week find that time to take care of you.

I am a Believer.

31 MICHELLE L. | DISCOVERING THE TRUE ME

There is more and more talk nowadays of the need to be true to yourself. The moment a person decides to start down the path of self-discovery, a journey begins of becoming aware of your true potential, your character, your motives and so on. I began to take the journey a few years ago.

For a long time, I lived with something called unawareness towards my true self. It was my time to find the purpose in my life and reveal experiences that shaped me to the person I am today. The effects of this self-discovery included happiness, self-realization, clarity and maybe even better insight! Taking this journey was not always an easy road because it included fear, confusion, misunderstanding, doubt and reassessing all the choices made in my life. It was like "spring-cleaning" of the mind, my emotions and surroundings including the people in my life. This process required making some tough decisions and sticking to them.

During my personal journey, I began to dig deep into my childhood. I can honestly say I had a good childhood, hard-working parents and was taught if you wanted something you had to earn it or eventually work for it. It is me and my brother, I am the oldest. It seemed my brother had it a little bit easier. Even today, in our 50's my brother is the "golden child" to my mom. I have a great relationship with my parents and brother, but I did realize deep down that "golden child" reference really bothered me, and I felt I had to work hard for my mother's acceptance even though that wasn't the case. She was proud of me but didn't voice it to me like she would to my brother.

In the middle of growing up with the "golden child" times, I eventually began dating at the age of 18, and was in a verbally abusive 8-year relationship which was on and off again. I would always go back because I didn't think that anyone else would ever want me. I lacked confidence and struggled with my appearance. I was always told by my boyfriend that nobody would ever like me and constantly trying to pretend I was happy and truly was not.

But there came a day when I finally had enough, and I remember it as plain as day. I decided to leave the relationship for good. Best decision I ever made. I would say that day was a big turning point in my life. I started to think about me and my direction in life. I learned what I would not accept in a relationship and grew stronger and more confident about myself.

I did finally get married to someone and the marriage had its ups and downs. The best thing out of the marriage was my daughter, my only child. She is my world and in college. There were struggles with her as well because she had ADD. But back then getting the schools to admit that was what she had wasn't easy. By the time she was in 5th grade, I was at wits end. I was the one that worked with her on homework and made sure it was always done. It was not easy, she would throw the books, break the pencils, leave the table and dance around etc. Homework that should have taken 30 minutes was more like 2 hours.

She excelled working one on one with someone. So that was a lot of money for no diagnosis. I then took her to Child Behavioral Psychologist who did diagnose her after tests with low to moderate

ADD. Amen, I thought. I'm not crazy. She was put on medication, but she was fine for a while and then when the medication wore off, she was a monster. I did a lot of research on my own and found a medication that works with the body chemically and releases as needed.

Once my daughter was put on that, she was a whole different person. She remained on the Honor Roll all through elementary and high school. She thrives at college and her medication has been reduced significantly now that she is older. I did not give up on her, my husband didn't want her on any medication and was fighting me the whole time, but I held my ground. What did he know he was never home during homework time because he worked the 3rd shift so he was sleeping when I was working with her?

During all this time and to this day, I continue to work on myself and I decided to look at the people in my life. There were people in my life, I called "takers." They were takers because I allowed them to make me feel guilty and bad about myself. I suddenly came to the realization that I needed to get rid of them. I no longer have expectations from others, well most of the time. Once I made this change, the course of my life continued in its positive direction.

I began to follow my true passion and purpose. I've had several setbacks along the way, and I have no doubt I will have many more but, I'm not giving up on me.

What I know for sure is that I have been very hard on myself for most of my life. I have not been truthful with myself and have had unrealistic expectations therefore, setting myself up for disappointment. There comes a freedom with accepting your feelings and emotions. It's like a release of some sort. Like you've identified the elephant in the room and waved at him, so you no longer must pretend he's not there.

Once you acknowledge the elephant in the room, he doesn't bother you anymore. You learn to co-exist and be okay with his presence and not allow him to control how you act and feel anymore.

I know for sure is that we are usually our own worst enemy. We keep ourselves back in so many ways and I am ready to move away from that model. I'm not suggesting that these fears no longer exist within me because they certainly do and, I don't think they will ever go away, but now that I am aware of my true feelings and now that I am becoming conscious of my true beliefs, they no longer have a stifled hold on my life.

Here's the message to all of you reading this. Stop being your own worst enemy! Stop lying to yourself about your passions and feelings and start accepting them. Allow yourself to feel whatever is it you feel. The freedom you will feel within yourself is reward enough however, the universe will give you back the love that you have finally and rightly provide to give yourself. Begin to believe in yourself, it is then that you will become unstoppable.

You will BECOME "YOU".

You will BECOME a Selfish B.

31 SUSAN FRONGILLO | I TOOK CONTROL

"Look at your stomach sticking out, you would look so pretty if you lost some weight."

My aunt was being candid, and I was only eight years old. I often wondered why I looked the way I did. I wondered if this was the reason why I was always picked last or close to last at recess. That feeling of rejection each time you lined up for teams to be chosen, still haunts me. I did not want to be the last to be picked any longer. As I got older, I fought hard to overcome my weight and I maintained a generally more slender figure until the age of 20 when I became pregnant with my son.

During my pregnancy, my doctor advised me to eat anything I wanted, and boy did I ever! After I gave birth, I pumped breastmilk for my son for a year and put off dieting of any kind. My life became focused on my baby. I knew that if I was a good mom and worked hard, I could afford a good lifestyle for my son and that was all that mattered.

One day I finally went for a physical and my doctor questioned why I had not been in to the office in several years. I responded with, "I have been busy with my son." She reminded me that in order to be a good parent, I needed to ensure I would be here for the long term for him. This moment was my epiphany. I didn't want my son to grown up without me. I knew all too well the pain and void of losing a parent as my father had passed suddenly when I was a sophomore in high school. I had never imagined he wouldn't be there for me for the long term. I knew in that moment that I needed to do all I could not only for my son, but for myself to ensure I would be here in the future.

Luckily, my only official diagnosis on this day– obesity. So, there I was at 190 pounds and barely five feet tall and classified as obese. The next day, I took control, and jumped right in to a healthy eating plan. I began to eat a typical healthy diet and worked out five days a week. I was on a mission. With a lot of hard work and determination, I managed to get my weight down to 143 pounds. Although this weight was more desirable, I was still considered overweight, and the weight loss did not last very long.

I was soon back up to that 190 number! In 2011, I was desperate and started playing with different foods. I was convinced that while exercise was important, diet played a huge role.

Luckily enough, food has always been a passion in my life. A burning passion. The type of passion where you would cook a gourmet meal on a Tuesday night because, why not? I have always loved cooking. I love the satisfied faces of people whom ate my food. I also enjoyed being able to quickly make people happy through the meals I created. In my professional world it often takes a month or more to make a customer happy by closing on a home. Luckily with cooking, the satisfaction is instantaneous. Since cooking food came easy to me, I played with different varieties of foods, in fact, I started to eat only protein and fat (eggs and a breakfast meat), lunch would be a salad or sandwich, and dinner consisted of mostly protein and fat again. This diet and way of eating basically began to work wonders for me.

I had lost about 40 pounds, but I was at a plateau and I wanted to solve it through food. I cut back on my carbs even further and this put my body into ketosis. Ketosis occurs when your body lacks carbohydrates and uses its own fat for energy. I started getting hooked to this way of dieting. I was losing weight, not hungry and things were looking good again. The day the scale broke 143, I knew I had something good going on. I watched my weight creep down lower and lower. Could I really break 130? I think I was 135 when I graduated high school! Before I knew it, not only did I break 130, but with dedication, the scale descended further and further. People started noticing and I was so happy that I had finally found something that worked.

Gone were the days, when I would spend hours to try to find something to wear that did not make me look "fat," and the nights when I stayed in crying because I felt horrible in my own wardrobe. As I got thinner, people often asked me at what point was I going to "stop dieting". I was obsessed with losing weight, but I did not stop the diet until I weighed 105 pounds and was a size 00. My goal was not to maintain at this weight but give myself a cushion in the event it started to creep back up again.

According to the dreaded BMI chart, I maintained a healthy weight until I delivered my next baby. Yes, almost two decades later, I delivered my second child. Ironically, I gained again to that awful number of 190. This time, I knew exactly what to do to lose the baby weight and nothing was going to stand in my way.

In September of 2016, I jumped into ketosis! This time my son who wanted to also focus on getting healthier, joined me and we supported one another in our goas. Within six months, my son and I lost 70 pounds each. He was on a college budget, and I was cooking family meals. This time around, I noticed that this eating lifestyle was gaining popularity and it was both positive and negative. Sure, there were more food options and opinions, but I had to stay true to what worked for me, real whole foods.

In order to sustain this long term, I wanted to make sure that my fiancé and family ate great meals, but I was not about to cook two dinners. The goal was to figure out a way to continue to cook the meals my family loved, but they needed to support my weight loss goals.

Born was the keto cookbook. I basically cooked my normal meals but keto style. I desperately wrote down recipes to remember for future times I wanted to cook the same thing. Recipe writing is against my nature because I love to be inventive and not follow a script. My recipes have always lived in my head and putting them on paper seemed a bit artificial and forced for me.

I am currently pushing to get the cookbook published by next year. So many people comment, "Susan you are such an inspiration, I could never have that much willpower" I want those who struggle with their weight to know that they can still eat tasty, fulfilling dinners and like the lifestyle that works for me, they too can find one that works for them.

We may have similar weight loss struggles, but we are all different. How our bodies respond to certain foods is something unique to each of us. I am proud that I found something that my body responds to and my advice to anyone reading this is to never give up on your weight loss journey or your goals to get healthy.

You will find something that works for you.

For the first time in so long I can say confidently that

I am a **Beauty**.

GINA CLAPPROOD

A NEW BREED OF B'S

We have struggled. We have taken risks. We have taken leaps of faith. We have learned lessons. We are strong. We have persevered. We are empowered.

We have committed to our health. We have committed to our happiness. We have selfishly committed to ourselves. We have kept our sanity.

We have gone against the norm. We have done the unexpected. We have broken the rules. We have set examples.

We have loved. We have lost. We have survived.

We have said "No" to the status quo. We have fought for what we believe in. We have owned our true selves.

We are Selfish B's: We are Beauties. We are Bitches. We are Bosses. We are Bachelorettes, Brides and Baby Mamas. We are believers. We are Badasses.

We are the new breed of B's – The Queen Bs…and these are our comebacks.

ABOUT THE AUTHOR

An Intuitive Lifestyle Coach and Advisor for more than 20 years, Gina provides support and insight to help other achieve their goals, make real changes, and become their ultimate selves. Always a thoughtful listener, Gina was recognized as highly intuitive from an early age and over the years has learned to channel this skill to give back to others. Experienced in working with all ages, stages of life and levels of success, she helps people through the challenges of life in concrete ways.

Through her work with others, Gina found commonalities with her clients, family and friends regarding the guilt they would feel when they thought about putting themselves first. Whether they were single, married, moms, bosses, etc. Gina found that she would give similar advice in each situation- and the idea for this book was born.

Gina is a promoter of believing in oneself and writes and speaks about the mindset needed for self-love.

Married to her high school sweetheart and the mother of three boys, she is based in Rhode Island and works with everyone from A-listers to longtime clients all over the world.

Your review is so much appreciated on <u>Amazon</u>!

To connect with Gina: www.ginaclapprood.com

Instagram: @your_life_styled

Join the Selfish B's on Facebook and share your story @thequeenbbook + Instagram @thequeenb_book

For book tour information, speaking engagements + all other inquiries: theselfishb@gmail.com

Made in the USA
Middletown, DE
10 February 2019